Taking Inquiry Outdoors

Reading, Writing, and Science Beyond the Classroom Walls

Edited by Barbara Bourne

**Elementary Science Integration Project,
University of Maryland Baltimore County**

Stenhouse Publishers
Portland, Maine

Stenhouse Publishers
www.stenhouse.com

Copyright © 2000 by Stenhouse Publishers

Library of Congress Cataloging-in-Publication Data
Taking inquiry outdoors : reading, writing, and science beyond the classroom walls / edited by Barbara Bourne.
p.   cm.
Includes bibliographical references (p.   )
ISBN 1-57110-302-3
1. Natural history—Study and teaching (Elementary) Anecdotes. 2. Natural history—Study and teaching (Elementary) I. Bourne, Barbara.
QH51.T35   1999
372.3'57—dc21
99–33923 CIP

Cover and interior design by Joyce C. Weston
Cover photograph by Barbara Bourne

Manufactured in the United States of America on acid-free paper
05 04 03 02   9 8 7 6 5 4 3 2

Taking Inquiry Outdoors

Contents

Acknowledgments

The material in this volume is based upon work supported by the National Science Foundation under grant number TPE-9353454. Any opinions, findings, and conclusions or recommendations expressed in this material are those of the authors and do not necessarily reflect the views of the National Science Foundation.

The authors of this book are all participants or staff of the Elementary Science Integration Project (ESIP), a teacher-enhancement project sponsored by the University of Maryland Baltimore County. ESIP is a collegial network of educators who seek to link authentic science with reading, writing, and other curricular areas. Those interested in learning more about ESIP can call the ESIP office at 410-455-2373 or visit the program's web site at http://www.umbc.edu/esip.

Our thanks to Donna Neutze for her bibliographic research and patient proofreading of many documents, sometimes several times over.

About the Contributors

Barbara Bourne is the Program Director of the Elementary Science Integration Project (ESIP) at the University of Maryland Baltimore County. She has written chapters, articles, and teachers' guides, and is coauthor of *Exploring Space: Using Seymour Simon's Astronomy Books in the Classroom* (Morrow Junior Books 1994) and *Thinking Like Mathematicians: Putting the K–4 NCTM Standards into Practice* (Heinemann 1994).

Deborah Galinksi has been teaching at the elementary level for nine years and currently teaches third grade in Carroll County, Maryland. She has conducted numerous workshops on taking inquiry outdoors for the Elementary Science Integration Project.

Mary Beth Johnson teaches fourth grade at Beall Elementary School in Montgomery County, Maryland. For four years she taught a science lab for 650 students in grades K–5 and developed outdoor science programs as well as curricula that linked reading and science. She is one of the contributors to *Beyond the Science Kit: Inquiry in Action*, edited by Wendy Saul and Jeanne Reardon (Heinemann 1996).

Karen Pearce is a middle school language arts and reading teacher at West Middle School in Carroll County, Maryland. She and her husband have taught several ESIP courses that focus on using the outdoors as an authentic setting for integrating science and language arts. Their daughter and son-in-law join them as active participants.

Brenda Picarello has taught in Baltimore County Maryland Public Schools since 1985. She taught pre-kindergarten for seven years and is currently the library media specialist at Timonium Elementary School. Brenda continues to learn about the wonders of the world through the eyes of children, particularly her own boys, Bryan and Jeffrey.

Michael Rest began his teaching career at Harlem Park Elementary School in Baltimore, Maryland. After teaching for a year in South Korea,

Mr. Rest returned to Baltimore City Public Schools as a sixth-grade science teacher at Harlem Park Middle School. He continues to be actively involved in the community.

Sharon Robinson-Boonstra has been a science educator for twenty years and currently teaches Life Science and Earth Science to seventh- and eighth-grade students at the Key School in Annapolis, Maryland. Outdoor environmental study has been an integral component of her science curriculum for the past nine years.

Lorraine Russo has taught first grade for fifteen years in the New York and Maryland public school systems. She currently teaches first grade at Burtonsville Elementary School.

E. Wendy Saul is Professor of Education at the University of Maryland Baltimore County and the principal investigator of the Elementary Science Integration Project and *Find It! Science,* a CD-ROM-based product that guides users in selecting science-related trade books. Dr. Saul has edited, written, and contributed to a number of books including *Beyond the Science Kit: Inquiry in Action* (Heinemann 1996) and *Science Workshop: A Whole Language Approach* (Heinemann 1993).

Karen Shrake is a fourth-grade teacher at Burtonsville Elementary School in Montgomery County, Maryland, and has co-authored an article, "Literature Study Groups: An Alternative to Ability Grouping," that was published in *The Reading Teacher* (April 1991). She was the Maryland recipient of the Presidential Award for Excellence in Science Teaching in 1997.

CHAPTER 1

So This *Is Science!*

BARBARA BOURNE

I NEVER LIKED science as a child—or so I thought. It was, in a word, boring. I preferred the out-of-doors to the classroom; was far more attached to exploration than memorization.

My fondest childhood memories are of the out-of-school hours I spent with my brother, unlocking the mysteries of the woods and streams behind our home. We knew each tree intimately—which ones were the sturdiest for tree houses; which were too sticky with pitch to climb while wearing school clothes; and which lost their leaves too early in the fall to provide sufficient camouflage for secret meetings.

Our clothes were perpetually muddy and our shoes forever wet. In the spring we collected tadpoles in our grandmother's old enamel tub and tracked the survivors' metamorphosis into tiny frogs that we released back into the wild. We devised elaborate plans to change the course of nature, but continually discovered that we were no match for the immutable forces we worked so hard to alter. Many hours were spent trying to straighten the course of a meandering stream. Many days were spent trying to dam that stream into a pond. And many dimes were spent at Woolworth's before we realized that ten-cent goldfish just weren't going to survive in cold Massachusetts waters.

Regular Saturday excursions to nearby beaches provided us with a comfortable familiarity of the shoreline—with snails, crabs, and sand dollars; with wind, waves, and the therapeutic (but painful) effect of salt water on that week's newest crop of bug bites and poison ivy. After autumn and winter storms, we'd return to the beach and marvel at the strength and fury displayed by the very same ocean we'd playfully splashed in a few months before.

When family trips and outdoor play ceased to be "cool," I went off to summer camp, where I found a built-in cohort of fellow adventurers to share in an ever-widening exploration of our outdoor home. We lived in the woods. We canoed each cove and inlet. We climbed New England's tallest mountain and threw snowballs near its summit in July. We fell asleep under the stars and, damp with dew, awoke to the sounds of the birds. Our shared experience of living outdoors not only forged lifelong friendships, it also cemented a lifelong love of the natural world.

But carefree summers inevitably led to routine Septembers and the return of textbooks and tests. When well-meaning adults pulled out that standby conversation starter, "What's your favorite subject in school, dear?" my reply was quick and well rehearsed. "I'm not sure, but I know what I don't like—science!" My later school experiences did nothing to contradict my early impressions, and I took pride in the growing number of science classes I *didn't* take while completing school.

Little did I realize the depth of my naturally acquired understanding, the intimate knowledge I'd gained of the world, or the authenticity of my scientific experiences. Little would I have predicted that as an adult I'd be fascinated with the very subject I'd avoided for so long and even end up working in a program with the word "science" in its title.

Coming Home to Science

The Elementary Science Integration Project (ESIP) has offered a home to many unrealized scientists like myself, adults who for years have avoided taking or teaching science, but who nonetheless nurture a lifetime of scientific experience. In ESIP, teachers with expertise in science work alongside those whose strengths are in language arts and literature as together they explore the connections of science to their own lives and its potential impact on their classroom practice.

Second-grade teacher Debora Lang referred to her ESIP experience as an opportunity to find her "science self." This personal journey moved Debora from being simply a language/literature/arts-focused teacher to being a more science-focused *person*. Her interests were sparked during an ESIP institute of inquiry and reflection and then nurtured by travel and reading—and by exploring the world of science alongside her students.

Over the past nine years, ESIP records have documented how a large number of participants have turned to the outdoors as a comfortable place to begin their entry into classroom science. Perhaps they do so because they, too, harbor an unrealized "science self," one that is already in tune with the science and aesthetics of the natural world.

Betty Lobe, a twenty-three-year teaching veteran, is representative of the many ESIP participants who, on entering the program, viewed themselves as "very knowledgeable" in the teaching of reading, writing, social studies, and/or the arts, but saw themselves as "weak" in the sciences. It's interesting to note that although Betty's ESIP application stated numerous times and in numerous ways that she did not view herself as competent in science, she actually did possess a wealth of scientific interest and knowledge. She'd taken several outdoor education courses and, along with her husband, was a bird-watcher and a member of the local zoological society.

Furthermore, it was clear from her application that she already valued the qualities necessary for teaching science in the classroom. "I am more patient, more thoughtful, more reflective, more of a guide on the side," she wrote. "My confidence allows me to not have all the answers, therefore I am a listener . . . I enjoy teaching more than ever because it has become a great adventure for me."

Despite her underlying knowledge and interest, Betty's venture into the world of science loomed as a personal challenge. She struggled with her identity as a scientist and as a science teacher during her first ESIP summer but, as the following journal entries reveal, she gradually began to recognize her own "science self" hidden within the love of nature that emerged as her first comfort zone. Taking children outdoors became a starting place for science in her classroom.

July 12, 1996

I do not think of myself as a scientist and I feel very uncomfortable teaching science. However, I feel that changing. I love the out-of-doors and nature and have taken outdoor education courses. When I pair that knowledge with all the wonderful books that you surround us with, I immediately feel more comfortable.

I do and can do journal writing. I can take my students for nature walks and have them respond in writing. I can get copies of Jean Craighead George's books, in fact, I've already read some and in the 5th grade we [study] ecosystems. I've already arranged for the entire 5th grade to board various boats with the Living Classroom Foundation. I have a willingness and a desire and now I need to learn how to set the stage to provide my students with the opportunities and skills to format and investigate the questions I know they have.

July 16, 1996

I [am] more aware of my need to bring science home to my own backyard and theirs. I keep thinking of the . . . tree outside of my classroom. We sit under it to read and write, we predict the dropping of its beautiful leaves, we watch the birds at rest in its boughs and take beautiful pictures of ourselves under it, but I bet none of us knows its name.

I guess that is where authentic inquiry comes into play. That tree is really important to me and my kids in many ways and it would be easy to incorporate that tree into my ecosystems unit. I need to bring it home. If my science is to be rigorous and relevant, I need to bring it home.

The science in Betty's classroom was indeed rigorous and real as it took dramatic turns the next school year. September began with simple explorations of their schoolyard habitat, but students' questions soon took off in multiple directions, weaving in and out of the mandated curriculum. In an end-of-year journal entry, Betty reflected on the work the class had done.

May 10, 1997

Mornings before school are periods of rush and confusion for many of my students, so I chose to begin each day with a Native American tale. It began our thinking in terms of Mother Earth and because we were scientifically exploring our school grounds, it appeared to be a thought-provoking, yet calming, way to begin our day . . .

The gathering for me [started as] an attempt to build community within my group and allowed me to move quietly into the background. It became much more. I saw it emerge as a clearinghouse for ideas, spark new investigations, and become our classroom think-tank. The students began to share their own reading selections and their investigations. During the unstructured moments (break, transition, recess) everyone was busily engaged in meaningful activity. Students were investigating their own questions and these 5th grade students exhibited that remarkable gift of child-like wonder . . .

"To thine own self be true and then as sure as night follows the day, thou cannot be false to any man." That schoolyard was my security blanket in those early months. I loved the out-of-doors, had taken outdoor education classes and felt it was the natural setting for me to investigate and explore with my students.

Science from Nature: Starting as a Child

Coming to science through outdoor exploration seems a natural thing to do—especially for a child. Some would argue that a comfort with nature is inborn. In fact, noted naturalist E. O. Wilson has coined the term "biophilia" for that innate love of nature and affinity for other forms of life. In his autobiography he describes his own childhood exploits and explorations of the world around him as critical to his development as a naturalist and writer. After giving detailed accounts of his childhood encounters with various creatures of the sea, Wilson writes:

Why do I tell you this little boy's story of medusas, rays, and sea monsters, nearly sixty years after the fact? Because it illustrates, I think, how a naturalist is created. A child comes to the edge of deep water with a mind prepared for wonder . . . The waterland was always there, timeless, invulnerable, mostly beyond reach, and inexhaustible. The child is ready to grasp this archetype, to explore and learn, but he has few words to describe his guiding emotions. Instead he is given a compelling image that will serve in later life as a talisman, transmitting a powerful energy that directs the growth of experience and knowledge. (Wilson 1994, pp. 11–12)

Unlike E. O. Wilson, many of us (Betty and myself included) weren't encouraged to make those connections between "real science" and the less academic pursuits of a home-grown naturalist: sloshing through streams and then stooping to inspect an egg sac floating on the surface; quietly watching birds and building a familiarity with their habits and songs; relishing that musky, morning aroma that arises from a damp woodsy floor. Rather than recognizing the importance of science in our lives, we tended to recoil from anything "scientific" and believed that *we* didn't have the stuff of scientists, nor were we capable of sharing science with others.

Rachel Carson addressed this dilemma in her final book, *The Sense of Wonder:* "The lasting pleasures of contact with the natural world are not reserved for scientists, but are available to anyone who will place himself under the influence of earth, sea, and sky and their amazing life" (1956, p. 95). Carson recognized children's inborn curiosity and awe over the natural world, but also understood that the excitement can fade as children mature into adults. "If a child is to keep alive his inborn sense of wonder," she writes, "he needs the companionship of at least one adult who can share it, rediscovering with him the joy, excitement and mystery of the world we live in" (p. 45).

The teachers who contributed to this book have taken on Rachel Carson's challenge. They have moved beyond the classroom walls and are providing their students with authentic, real-world experiences. Some of the teachers have tapped into a lifelong love of nature while others are venturing out for the very first time, sharing the initial wonder of discovery right alongside their students. The children, in turn, are the direct beneficiaries of their teachers' evolving connection with the natural world. Going outdoors is immediate and real; it sparks questions; it offers avenues of exploration and investigation; and it is available, at little or no expense, to everyone.

The stories in this book are about more than just stepping out the door, more than simply letting children interact with the flowers, trees, and the great and small creatures of their neighborhoods. To twist a well-worn phrase from Henry David Thoreau's *Walden,* these chapters are documentaries of how teachers and students go to the woods (and the ponds, streams, and fields) to learn deliberately and to confront the essential facts of life. Children who go outside regularly begin to notice the cycles and patterns of nature, the habits of animal life, the beauty of the world around them. Learning from routine outdoor experience is not just deliberate, it is natural. It balances the intentional with the casual, the planned and the serendipitous. It builds on children's intrinsic curiosity and their need to interact with real objects and events.

Nature and Inquiry: Natural Connections

Questioning, exploring, investigating, manipulating, problem solving, communicating, reinventing understanding: these are the hallmarks of childhood—and they are the processes of scientific inquiry. The struggle to make meaning of the world begins in infancy and, for some at least, never ceases. Inquiry is a valuable means of addressing children's learning needs within the classroom. In fact, "Science as Inquiry" is the very first content standard for all grade levels (K–4, 5–8, and 9–12) as established by the *National Science Education Standards* (1996). For example, here is how the K–4 Inquiry Content Standards begin:

> From the earliest grades, students should experience science in a form that engages them in the active construction of ideas and explanations and enhances their opportunities to develop the abilities of doing science ... As students focus on the processes of doing investigations, they develop the ability to ask scientific questions, investigate aspects of the world around them, and use their observations to construct reasonable explanations for the questions posed. Guided by teachers, students continually develop their science knowledge. (p. 121)

Children in the classrooms featured in this book are engaged in the very processes the *Standards* advise. They are constructing ideas and formulating explanations. They are honing their abilities to ask scientific questions through direct observations of the world around them. They are using their observations to construct reasonable explanations and revisiting the objects of their investigations over the course of time. But these events don't "just happen."

Structuring Inquiry

Inquiry science is often associated with a lack of student accountability, with little teacher planning, and with scant attention to, or correspondence with, student learning outcomes. Fear of chaos, confusion, and disorder keeps many teachers from inviting inquiry into their classrooms and many administrators from encouraging its use in their schools.

ESIP teacher Susan Wells first began experimenting with classroom inquiry in 1992 and was initially very reluctant to let her students identify and explore questions that were important to them. Gradually, she found strategies that allowed her students to explore their own questions, that let her maintain a level of accountability, and that helped all of them to move through—and beyond—the district's curriculum. Susan's inquiry-based program of study addressed all of the science and many of the language arts, social studies, and mathematics outcomes called for in the curriculum. "Over the years," Susan explained in a recent workshop, "I found myself becoming *less controlling* and *more structured*." By imposing a structure on their students' inquiry experiences, Susan and other teachers are making sure these young scientists have the opportunity to make meaning of the science they are encountering.

In structured inquiry, both indoors and out, children are encouraged to investigate the questions that are important to them, but they are also required to meet certain guidelines before, during, and after their period of investigation. Every student needs a plan before starting. They all must be able to articulate *what* they are doing and *why* they are doing it during their investigation time.

Science in these classrooms is more than just "doing," more than "hands-on." Students write, read, listen, and share their discoveries and questions with others. Notes are kept, data collected, questions recorded, and observations documented. At the completion of each day's work, the class might convene in a scientists' meeting, where student-scientists share the results of a single or ongoing investigation. Other students respond to the data and conclusions and may offer suggestions or new questions to explore. This discourse helps children critically review their own experiences, place these experiences within the larger context of group findings, evaluate and compare data, generalize concepts, and, best of all, come up with new questions to explore.

Outdoor Inquiry: More Than a Breath of Fresh Air

Science in the out-of-doors must be held to the same standards as science conducted within the school building. There should be a plan and there should be a purpose. ESIP teacher Jeanne Reardon states in *Beyond the Science Kit: Inquiry in Action* (1996) that the science in her classroom must be "real, relevant, and rigorous" (p. 18). Few experiences are more real and relevant than taking children outside to explore their immediate environment, but it takes careful planning by teachers to ensure that outdoor experiences incorporate rigorous science. A trip to the pond or a walk in the woods might be fun, but it is little more than a breath of fresh air if children are not given the tools to make meaning of their experiences.

On the same day that I joined Lorraine Russo's students on the first of their weekly trips to a local lake, a colleague told me that she'd also joined a first-grade class on a nature walk. She was disappointed that the student teacher hadn't felt the need to make plans beyond sending home permission slips and arranging for chaperones. The children held hands, walked through the woods, and collected some leaves and pinecones to add to their "nature table." There was no advance preparation and little follow-up when they returned to the classroom. The children had a great time, but they weren't encouraged to make any new meaning of their natural world as they walked and talked.

Lorraine Russo (see Chapter 2) began preparing her first graders for their trips to the pond weeks in advance. After a brief visit to the school's courtyard, she realized that five- and six-year-olds needed to practice the skills that would make them successful scientists at the lake. They learned to sit quietly so they wouldn't trample the plants or chase away the insects and birds they'd come to observe. They practiced looking at tiny details and listening for quiet sounds. They learned how to collect data, they read books about pond life, and they collected the tools and supplies they would need to conduct their investigations.

Like all the teachers featured in this book, Lorraine had no idea what her students' questions would be, how their investigations would evolve, or how the children would communicate their findings. But she had a substantive plan in place that was designed to support her students' emerging inquiry. As you'll read in her chapter, Lorraine's plan continually evolved, shifting to reflect the needs of the students and their investigations. It encompassed all content areas and involved her first graders in reading, writing, collecting and working with numbers, and studying the world around them.

Teachers' Critical Inquiry

This is not a book about environmental education, a how-to primer on conducting nature walks and stream studies, or a cookbook of recipes for integrating reading and writing tasks with earth science units. Readers might notice that some chapters don't even mention taking children outdoors until several pages in. That's because this is a book of reflections on children and learning; on teaching; on science made understandable through reading, writing, and hands-on investigations—all within the context of the outdoors. The classroom teachers who share their stories in this book are not just promoting inquiry-based learning for their students, they are also making critical inquires into their own teaching practices.

Sharon Robinson-Boonstra, a middle school teacher with an expertise in experimental science, worries how she can align her environmental and earth science units more closely with the models of authentic scientific inquiry she learned in the lab. Her moment of discovery—her "Aha!"—prompted her to see science in a whole new light.

Karen Pearce, a middle school English teacher who has a long-standing love of both nature and literature, articulates her reasons for regularly linking reading, writing, and science, especially in outdoor settings. At a time when many educators are inclined to increase reading instruction at the expense of science and other content-area subjects, Karen uses one subject area to enhance the other, welcoming the spark of inquiry and the aesthetics of nature into her language arts curriculum.

Brenda Picarello admits that she accepted a pre-kindergarten teaching position in part because it would not involve science teaching—or so she thought. But Brenda redefined her notions of science over the years, and became increasingly comfortable with not "knowing it all." She writes two parallel stories for this book: a diary of personal growth as teacher and scientist and a tale of very young children engaged in the dual processes of science-skill and language development.

Karen Shrake writes about the power of collegiality among teachers. Deborah Galinski wonders how the strategies she uses in the school*room* can support purposeful learning in the school*yard*. Lorraine Russo worries about the "wanderers," those children who rarely come up with questions or are unable to direct their own learning. As she moves a successful activity from one school to another, Mary Beth Johnson shares her ideas on planning: what to keep, what to pitch, what to modify, and what to add. Michael Rest writes of how he discovered teaching—not just the profession, but the craft.

Wendy Saul, who works regularly with classroom teachers and has an expertise in children's literature, describes how books have enhanced her appreciation and understanding of science and nature.

Outdoors is the common thread among these teacher stories. It serves as a natural setting for purposeful student learning and critical teacher reflection. The teachers who have contributed to this book regularly consider their own practice while engaging their students in "real, relevant, and rigorous" science throughout the year, both indoors and out. Books are readily available and used for many purposes in their classrooms: as introductions to new ideas, as tools for explaining difficult concepts, or simply as a good read. Writing is used not just as a means of reporting, but to introduce and reinforce the skills of professional scientists and writers: collecting and recording data, noting observations and changes over time, making work replicable for future scientists, communicating findings, thinking on paper and expressing ideas.

Why focus on taking children (and teachers) outdoors? What is it that invigorates children and invites even the most reluctant adults to step beyond the threshold of mortar and brick? Perhaps we have an inborn need to identify, and identify with, the flora and fauna around us. Maybe we are imprinted by those places where we first breathed fresh air or saw the sun rise, the moon glow.

Whatever the reason, we certainly trust the reality of the outdoors. We appreciate its importance to our own well-being and, without exaggeration, to the well-being of the planet. Outdoor experience is authentic. It has consequence. It provides a context for children and teachers who, like those of us who were unable to recognize the science in our own backyard explorations, are touched by the beauty, excitement, and the ongoing sameness and newness of the world in which we live.

CHAPTER 2

Fridays at the Lake

LORRAINE RUSSO

A S A TEACHER, I'm concerned about the children who don't have questions. What should I do to focus the wanderers? How can I guide children who seem unfocused without directing them or giving them my questions to investigate?

I didn't ask questions as a child, preferring instead to follow the lead of others, so at first the idea of teaching children to think for themselves was both unfamiliar and uncomfortable for me. I had always been directed in my own learning—told what to do, how to do it, where to go. Rarely was I in a position where someone expected me to *think,* let alone ask questions.

All that changed when I joined the Elementary Science Integration Project (ESIP), a program in which educators were not given *answers* for how to teach science, but were expected to come up with *questions* about science and about their own teaching practice. As participants in the program, we weren't given formulaic plans with which to develop lessons and units on electricity or ecology. We were given opportunities to explore batteries and bulbs or ponds and streams ourselves; encouraged to generate our own questions; and eventually driven to conduct our own research through reading, writing, collaboration, and authentic investigation. In other words, we engaged in our own inquiry-based activity and, in turn, learned how to involve our students in questioning, investigating, and communicating about the world around them.

I left the 1996 ESIP Summer Institute knowing I wanted the children in my class to wonder, think, question, explore, write, and talk about science. But how?

As I began to plan for the coming school year, I thought back over past experiences, reflecting on those times when I felt most successful as a teacher. Actually, I'd been growing in autonomy as a special education teacher for some time before returning to regular first grade. In special education I had had the freedom to deviate from the traditional lesson plan and could focus on what worked, what engaged the children in learning. I remembered that the days we disregarded the lesson plans usually worked much better than those in which we rigidly clung to a predetermined set of activities. Time on task was increased, attention was consistent, and motivation for everyone was remarkably high.

As I thought about it, I realized that on those special days, I wasn't telling the children what to think and do; they were telling me. My role changed from director to facilitator. The kids took the lead. They made the decisions about what to investigate and how to do it. I occasionally interrupted with a question about procedure, materials, or data collection, but more often I listened—*really* listened—to what the children were saying and thinking.

I thought about what areas of investigation piqued interest and provoked questions and realized that whether they were at home, in the classroom, or on the playground, many of the children's questions sprang from their curiosity about the environment. This made sense to me. The children were naturally curious about their neighborhood, and their conversations and actions told me that they wanted and needed time to explore, test, observe, and find answers to their own questions about the world around them. The opportunities for inquiry were readily available—I just had to be receptive and prepared for the teachable moments.

I armed myself with my emerging insights and convictions about science, teaching, questioning, and first graders and began to look for possibilities in the environment around the school. We had an open courtyard at our building that was home to a variety of trees, shrubs, flowers, and, in turn, numerous insects and birds. I discovered a small lake nearby and was sure that visits there would intrigue and inspire my first-grade scientists. But I had doubts. I wasn't sure how to get started. My experiences with nature were very limited, and I was concerned about accessibility, since I do most of my teaching from a wheelchair.

Then, in the very first week of school, a wonderful, unexpected teaching moment occurred—a unique opportunity that turned out to be not just a meaningful experience for my students, but a turning point for me. I was given a chance to move aside, to watch children work and make sense of their world, to think about inquiry and the excitement of discovery, and see firsthand how trusting children and letting them direct their own learning can bring great rewards to everyone.

Swept Up in a Storm of Excitement

Hurricane Fran. For a week the media had covered this major storm as it wound its way up the eastern shore of the United States. I paid little attention to it, being preoccupied with the business of starting a new school year and getting the class underway. But by Thursday evening, I couldn't avoid it. Local weather reports began predicting what effect the storm might have on the Chesapeake Bay region.

"Wow!" I thought. "These broadcasts really capture what a hurricane is like. I've got to show the kids!" I taped the news that night, bought a newspaper the next morning, and headed for school.

Film clips of the hurricane, weather maps, evacuation routes, emergency procedures, damage paths, and simulations of hurricane-force winds greeted the students as they arrived and unpacked their book bags. As the morning progressed, we read newspaper articles and looked at photos of the damage the storm had inflicted as it traveled up the coast. The children were mesmerized by all they heard and saw. They were excited and concerned. They talked and talked.

Suddenly the lights went out.

We were so wrapped up in our indoor discussion about the storm, nobody had noticed that outdoors the winds were kicking up and it had started to rain. Someone yelled, "It's here!" and we ran to the windows to watch.

The whole building was encased in darkness, but every eye in my classroom was focused on that storm. When we were told that despite the power outage, school would remain open, I decided to make the most of it. We would go outside to experience the storm up close (staying close to the building for safety).

What a fantastic, sensory experience! We felt the cold, wet raindrops on our faces and heard the roar of the wind in our ears. We noticed changes in the environment and started asking questions.

Dark, heavy clouds were moving rapidly across the sky. Why were the raindrops so scattered? Would we get heavier rains? Flocks of birds were leaving the trees. Were they going to a safer place? If so, where might that be?

Debris flew by. Where would it land? What kind of damage would it do?

The children talked and talked. The questions kept coming. Even after we returned to the classroom they continued to discuss the storm. I filled two large pieces of chart paper with their comments.

Did you see the birds leaving the trees? Where were they going?
The clouds were very black. I think it's gonna start raining.
The wind sounded really loud. I had to cover my ears.
The clouds were moving fast!

As we began to read back the sentences (by flashlight), Emily said, "The sentences are not in the right places. He's talking about the wind; I'm talking about the rain. We should put all the sentences together."

I was amazed. Just five days into the school year and these first graders were already looking to organize their data! How could I build on this turn of events?

I quickly cut the chart paper into sentence strips and handed them out, and the children organized themselves into groups by topic: rain, wind, storm, clouds, electricity. They read the sentences aloud (with a little help), but stopped yet again, this time because the sequence wasn't correct. They wanted the sentences to be read in the same order that the storm had occurred.

I watched and listened to the children as they rearranged themselves and realized that this was how they were making sense of the storm. In a way, they were recreating it on their own terms to better understand this remarkable force of nature. I was fascinated. What would come next? What else would I learn from these five- and six-year-olds that day?

They were not, in fact, finished with their work. Now they wanted to act it all out, to "be the hurricane." This was no easy task. Each child had his or her own ideas about the characteristics of the storm. There was a lot of confusion about what kind of storm the hurricane actually was, in part because so many children had seen the movie *Twister* and were confusing hurricanes with tornadoes.

Finally, I had an opportunity to introduce books into the discussion. The children could research their questions and back up their discussions with facts. I grabbed the flashlight and a book about storms. As I read, the children sat engrossed, waiting for information, not just to settle their disputes, but to enable them to go on with their hurricane plans. They were desperate to increase their level of knowledge so that they could continue their work. Their interests had driven them to research. I made a mental note always to have a wide variety of science trade books and materials available so we could take advantage of learning opportunities that spring up without warning.

The day moved on—and so did the children's hurricane activity. They were still anxious to act out the storm, but were unable to reach consensus on how it should be done. I wanted to intervene, take control of the situation, make a suggestion, but something told me to step back and let the kids handle it themselves. This was tough! Strong discussions ensued and a few arguments came up, but I held back. I knew that if the children were going to conduct their own investigations that year, problems like these would continually arise. I wanted my students to persevere and resolve issues not by deferring to me, but by discussing, trying new things, sharing ideas, *thinking*—to understand the importance of resourcefulness. I really wanted them to learn to value one another's ideas, and I knew that would not happen if they thought I had all the answers and could solve all the problems.

I was taking a risk by stepping back, and I wanted them to take some risks in working out their own questions. I stayed quiet but kept a watchful eye. After a few (stressful) minutes, the children came up with a plan acceptable to everyone. They'd created and produced an original "hurricane opera" and were so excited about their performance, they wanted to take it on the road to other classes. By then, however, it was lunchtime, and even opera stars have to eat, so we unpacked our lunches and relaxed from the whirlwind of the morning's activity.

Then, as we ate, a small voice said, "You know, we should make a book."

I was so surprised! I thought that by now they'd be tired of the hurricane and anxious to move on to something else. But they were completely committed to this investigation and wanted to continue. As they ate their lunches they began to discuss how to make the book. They decided where to put the pictures, text, and newspaper clippings. They debated titles, names, and who would do the coloring. All I could do was sit back and listen, remembering all those afternoons we felt forced into covering mandated curricula. Suddenly, it seemed so easy. Once the children took control of their own learning, motivation ceased to be a problem. Ownership gave them power and gave me opportunities to weave in literature, writing, and science.

After a day of darkness, I was beginning to see the light.

Coming Back Down to Earth

The experience with Hurricane Fran was the first time I truly saw myself more as a facilitator than a teacher, and even though I found it a little scary not being able to predict where my students' questions would lead and what would come out of their explorations, I was able to listen to the children and watch how their thinking evolved throughout the day. I saw how one event could stimulate ideas and spur investigations with minimal guidance from me. I was able to step back and let the students resolve their own problems. I maintained the structure within the classroom but handed the control over to the children and let their interests and questions drive that day's instruction. Because I had changed my teaching practices to accommodate for inquiry, the learning in our classroom had taken on a life of its own.

This was great. I was riding high from the success of that Friday, sure that I'd discovered the answer to incorporating inquiry into my regular classroom program. All I had to do was choose a topic that was intrinsically interesting, and my students would organize themselves into a meaningful learning activity. I listed topics I knew would spark interest among first graders and decided on "water." Yes, we'd explore water at our next inquiry session.

Friday arrived and I was ready. Each group of children, sitting at a table, got a tub of water and a variety of materials with which they could explore. Assured that they were able to investigate on their own, I gave minimal directions. Within ten minutes the desks, the carpet, and the children were soaked, the materials were destroyed, and the room was a mess.

What a disaster! I couldn't imagine where I'd gone wrong. Things had been so wonderful the week before—and with a lot less preparation.

I went home that night, not just wet, but thoroughly defeated. I mentally replayed the day's events over and over again, looking for indications of where things had fallen apart. Gradually, it occurred to me that I hadn't given the children any instructions on how to use the materials. I had assumed that they were familiar with the processes of systematic investigation and that they would come up with their own plans and strategies to explore water. I'd given them plenty of materials, but I had not given them the tools they needed to have a successful independent experience. I resolved to try again, but next time, I'd establish a structure through which the students would be able to conduct productive investigations.

I returned to my initial plans from the beginning of the year and decided to restart my classroom inquiry by taking the children outdoors. Here, everything was familiar, yet continually new. The children rarely tired of being outdoors, and I knew that afterward we could take their learning back indoors through reading and writing activities.

Before we began, I gathered the children around to discuss what had gone wrong the previous Friday. We brainstormed ideas about how to conduct investigations. I showed them how to use a magnifying lens to make things easier to see. Each child was given his or her own nature journal, clipboard, and pencil. Then, we spent some time predicting what we might see outdoors.

When we got out to the courtyard, the children immediately ran to all corners of the garden, journals and pencils in hand. I had a journal as well, but I was recording the children's comments and questions as they shouted across the courtyard. Michael immediately shouted that he had "found some kind of a nest," while Robby and Dana poked sticks into a storm drain, "looking for frogs." Elizabeth and Neisha followed a trail of ants with their magnifiers, hoping to "see how they walk." I planned to use this information later during our discussion time.

We found all sorts of interesting creatures that day, from birds to bugs to butterflies. Many of the children checked out the plants, trees, bushes, and flowers. Some focused on the sewer drain and wondered who or what might live there. One boy, much to my distress, put his hand in a wasp nest, but fortunately he wasn't stung. This led to lots of speculation as the children began to question their long-held ideas about wasps and bees.

The morning seemed perfect. The children were engaged in a variety of investigations and grew excited over their discoveries. But as I watched their frenzied activity and listened to their chatter, I realized that in all the excitement and noise, they were missing the opportunity to really see the garden and the workings of nature. I thought about the fact that children must be taught the processes of science: quiet observation, listening, watching—patience.

I asked them to sit on the ground, put their clipboards aside, and just listen. No talking. No poking. No running. It took a few minutes, but the birds that had flown out of the garden during our visit soon returned, swooping down into the trees around us. The bees went back to their flowers, and the children could hear them go bumbling by. A flock of geese honked as they flew overhead.

As we became silent, nature forgot that we were there. Its sounds filled the garden. Soon, the children picked up their journals and quietly recorded their observations. Some pieced together a few words and short phrases, but because these early first graders were emergent writers and readers, most drew pictures and diagrams of what they saw, sometimes labeling their illustrations with initial consonants.

How exciting! We were embarking upon a whole new level of nature study. As the children later shared their pictures and read the observations from their journals, I was struck by the detail with which they'd recorded their data. Was this because we had paused for a brief moment? Listened rather than spoke? Waited for the sounds of nature rather than giving voice to it ourselves?

Later, as I listened to their discussion and looked over their journals, I saw how their quiet observations had affected their thinking. The children had captured the essence of what was happening in the garden, and it was reflected in their conversation and their drawings.

Now I was really anxious to provide these budding scientists with further opportunities to sharpen their skills, knowing that it would spark future discussion, writing, and hopefully more questions. I planned to return to the garden with the children every week so that they could practice their emerging science-process skills as they observed the changes in nature over a period of time.

I was also committed to taking the children to the pond, but I knew we weren't quite ready. I was learning from the children in ways I would never have anticipated. Little did I expect that my next lesson would come from a young, timid child and his hermit crab from home.

Experts and Inquiry

It was early in the year and my first graders were still getting used to the routine of school. One student in particular was having a difficult time making the transition from the home to the school environment. To help him with the home-school transition, I asked his mother if there was anything he could bring in for show and tell, something he could share with the class that might make him want to come to school. We arranged for Sean to bring his hermit crab to school the next week.

The day arrived, and almost before Sean removed his crab from its cage, he was bombarded with questions. "What does it eat?" "How often?" "When?" "Does it make noise?" "Can he smell?" "How does it move?" "Can he change color?" "Can he swim?" "Does he drink water?"

Sean was in his glory. He was both the center of attention and the resident "crab expert." All of the children wanted to see and touch the crab, so I put the cage on a special table and established specific times when the children could observe him. (Sean was to be consulted first, of course.)

Suddenly, we were a class of crab researchers. The students drew pictures, wrote sentences, and read them aloud. They pored over books about crabs, both fiction and nonfiction. To learn more, they tested the crab with different foods and with water. They shared the results of their work with each other, made comments, and offered suggestions to their peers. Each time I turned around, they were talking about it. This crab was invading our lives!

And then it hit me: they *had* to keep talking to each other. They needed this forum to discuss what they'd observed, and if I wasn't going to give it to them on a regular basis, they were just going to take it for themselves, regardless of what else was going on in the classroom.

Once again, the children were "telling" me what they needed in a most effective way—by ignoring me and focusing on what was important to them.

This inquiry stuff was getting a bit tricky! I knew I had to give the children time to observe, explore, discuss, and write each time they were involved in an investigation. This need emerged early on, even with those first attempts at inquiry that I'd considered failures. But these processes take time—a lot of time. How was I going to work them into our weekly plans without cutting anything important out of the mix?

In addition, I was finally ready to begin weekly investigations at the lake, and I knew that those inquiry sessions would take even longer than the ones we'd conducted in the classroom. I was overwhelmed. I'd never taken students to a lake before. I didn't know what was going to happen or what investigations might develop. So, for the first time in my twelve years of teaching, I prepared no lesson plans for that Friday morning in late October. I simply wrote the word "lake" in my plan book. I didn't know what to expect. I just planned to rely on the structure set by previous inquiry experiences.

It's important to note that although I wrote no specific lessons for the day, I really knew I had to have a plan. I knew that "inquiry" did not mean "chaos," that relinquishing control did not imply losing focus. In fact, if ever I needed a structure to my day, it would be now when we were embarking on this extremely open-ended adventure. So even though I didn't know what to expect that first morning at the lake, I worked very hard at building a structure that would allow for productive inquiry.

To the Lake

We had begun our preparations for the excursion days in advance, making lists of what we'd need to bring with us in order to conduct our investigations. After looking at books, the children predicted the types of wildlife they thought they would see: geese, ducks, bugs, deer, fish, heron, beavers, turtles, butterflies, even foxes. On Friday, we packed a grocery cart full of tools—magnifiers, guides, buckets, thermometers, binoculars—and set off for the lake, full of excitement.

It was good that we were so prepared because the children were ready to launch their investigations as soon as we arrived. Several grabbed binoculars and started looking for wildlife. Some of the boys took hand lenses and nets and went off on their own to examine the grass for insects. A group of girls explored along the shoreline, poking into the mud where water meets land. A few more went right for the buckets and thermometers and quickly devised a way to test the temperature of the water beyond their reach. They tied the thermometers on strings and sticks and floated them a few feet from shore.

I was surprised to notice that, unlike previous class inquiries, these investigations were more individual. Each child seemed engrossed in what he or she was doing and was less interested than usual in communicating with the others.

But I needed to know more of what the children were doing, thinking, discovering. I had brought supplies with which to record questions and comments, and because the terrain wasn't accessible for my wheelchair, I had the children come to me to share their discoveries. To help elicit their ideas, I had made up rings of index cards for me and for the parents who ventured along. Each card displayed a question or prompt: What are you doing? What did you notice? What kind of test did you conduct? What surprised you? I referred to these questions while interviewing each child and recorded their responses on Post-it notes. I knew that in all the excitement, the children might forget what they'd seen and done, and I hoped that by referring back to my recorded notes I could help trigger their memories when it was time for a class discussion.

We spent over an hour at the lake that first day, then returned to school for a brief follow-up discussion. I was anxious to hear what the children had to say and how they would share their newly acquired information and questions. Imagine my disappointment when the main topic of discussion at this first "scientists' meeting" centered on a rusty old knife someone had retrieved from the water. There was plenty of speculation about the knife—how it got there, who it belonged to, what it did to the fish. The children were talking and questioning, but not in a direction I felt promoted scientific inquiry and investigation.

That's when I pulled out my ring of Post-it notes and "status of the class" sheets (Atwell 1987) on which I recorded children's comments. (See Figure 2.1.) I began to review what the children had noticed by reading what they had told me. For example, I would say, "Now, Denise, you mentioned that there were lots of mallards, but only five white ducks. Why do you think that is? How could you find out?" Questioning their observations seemed to give the children a jumping-off point, a place where they could start looking more closely and a means of helping them plan for our next visit to the lake.

As I flipped through my notes, I saw that I did not have comments from every child. Several of the children had not come to me at the lake or, if they did, they did not respond to my probes ("What are you doing?" "What did you notice?"). It was then that I realized that these were the same children who had been wandering around at the lake, not really focused on any investigation.

Here they were! The children I'd always feared—the ones with no apparent focus. These were the children who didn't have questions, the ones I worried about, the wanderers who needed direction. I couldn't

---

Figure 2.1. "Status of the Class" Sheet

Status of the Class

	Student			
1				
2				
3				
4				
5				
6				
7				
8				
9				
10				
11				
12				
13				
14				
15				
16				
17				
18				
19				
20				
21				
22				
23				
24				
25				
26				

imagine what I was going to do for these students and could only hope that I would figure it out as our investigations developed.

Our discussions continued after lunch. We took up our clipboards and paper, and the children and I began to draw and label some of our observations. I used large chart paper to model ways to record our discoveries. Many children drew their own versions, but some copied the information from my chart. I encouraged them to put in as many details as possible and was pleased when a few students added short sentences.

Many children began to talk as we worked. The drawing and writing freed them up and gave new life to our discussion. Suddenly, we were able to share our ideas and questions in a more productive fashion than we had during the morning's "rusty knife" discussion. Jonathan and Kenny told how they found "three different kinds of feathers—white, black, and brown"; Jennifer explained how she "made a fishing pole by tying a rock on the end so it would sink." Jamie said his thermometer went "all the way to 70 in the air," while Carrie reported that the water temperature was 50 degrees.

That night, I placed the sticky notes into a spiral notebook that I had set aside for data collection. (I wanted to be prepared with plenty of evidence of student learning and progress if I was ever questioned about the value of the lake activity.) As I reviewed the children's statements about what they had noticed, I gained new insights into what and how the children were thinking as well as what types of questions interested them. For instance, one child noticed that she saw more insects in the tall grass than in the short. Another said he had seen a "stingray." I realized that we needed to continue visiting the lake, hold more discussions, and conduct further research on pond life.

I was pleased with the children's observations, and planned to refer to them at the next scientists' meeting. But when I started to match my notes up with the students' names, I remembered that I did not have comments from everyone. I surely didn't know what everyone was thinking. How would I assess those students?

Focusing the Wanderers

The following Thursday afternoon, my first-grade scientists met with me in a pre-lake meeting. I couldn't wait to see what would happen. I had my trusty spiral notebook handy in case anyone forgot what he or she had explored the previous week. To get the discussion started I reminded them that we would be going to the lake the next day and I asked what they would be doing while there. At first, no one talked. I rekindled the discussion by referring to my notebook and soon, little by little, conversation developed.

The children talked, I recorded, and as they formulated their plans, I encouraged them to think about what tools and materials they would need to take with them to the lake. This was no easy matter, getting five- and six-year-olds to think ahead—to foresee what they must have in order to conduct their investigations. I certainly didn't want to tell them what to pack: I knew how important it was for them to figure it out on their own. So I had them role-play, act out their plans. To help them along, I asked questions: "How do you plan to do this?" "What will you use?" "How will you test that?" "What would help you find that information?"

Soon, they began to generate a list of supplies. I wrote the list on the chart so they could refer to it Friday morning while packing the cart. For example, Denise wanted to explore the tall grass, but hadn't been able to develop a list of supplies. Once she began to act out her intended investigation, she realized she needed to bring bug jars, sweep nets, and a magnifying glass. As she generated her list, other children began to think through their own investigations.

Things were really rolling now. Children were jumping in with suggestions about what they'd need and how they could conduct their experiments. Role-playing also helped them better plan their investigative approach. Some decided to work together; others preferred to go it alone. Everything was falling into place. Discussions were starting to take shape, plans were drawn up, materials were listed. Was this too good to be true?

Yes! Five of my students hadn't spoken a word—not one utterance, not one glimmer of participation. I quickly thumbed through my spiral notebook to see what they had been doing the week before. Of course— these were the children whose pages were blank. A familiar feeling of dread descended to the pit of my stomach. This was my point of panic, returning to haunt me—kids without questions.

"Think, think, think!" I kept telling myself. "There must be a way to get these kids involved." As I looked around the room to see what the other girls and boys were doing, I noticed small groups of children still chatting about their plans. I overheard one of them say, "Well, I'm going to find out how many birds there are."

Something clicked. Maybe I could use our "status of the class" sheets to keep track of what everyone was doing, and make sure they followed through. Maybe I could use accountability as a way to encourage my wanderers to find their path.

But how? It was twenty minutes before three and I had to bring closure to the meeting and get everybody packed up and on the bus by three o'clock. I hung the charts across the blackboard so everyone could see the different investigations that would take place the next day. Then, as I began to summarize who would be doing what, I heard myself saying, "And Bobby, you are going to look for animal tracks with Laura and Sean."

That's it, I thought. Everyone must have a reason, a purpose, for going to the lake; otherwise, why go? I made a point of moving around the room to review and confirm what everyone would be doing the next day. Then I addressed those girls and boys who had not yet shared any plans. "And why are you going to the lake tomorrow?" I asked each one. "What will you be doing?"

Of course none of them had a ready answer, so I followed up with, "Well, you need to think about what you'd like to do while you're there. You need to have a plan, some idea about what you'll be doing. And if you're not sure, then maybe you can work with another group and learn about their investigation. We all need to have an idea about what we'd like to do when we're there."

It rolled off my tongue as if the answer had been there all along and I just had to give it voice. I was making them accountable for themselves! I think that they may have gone into temporary shock, but my comments certainly got results. Two of the children decided to work independently, investigating insects. The other three decided to join in other groups' investigations. Now everyone had a plan. Everyone was accountable—and with ten minutes to spare!

From then on, things really took off. The children wanted to discuss their investigations throughout the week, so we began to hold scientists' meetings more often. I noticed that as they became more comfortable speaking about their work, the level and detail of relevant information increased dramatically.

Writing Like Scientists

The children were beginning to talk like scientists. They were able to describe their investigations and share collected data. They had been drawing conclusions based on their observations, tests, and readings like scientists. Now they were communicating like scientists.

Unfortunately, they were not writing like scientists. The entries in their science journals (booklets with blank pages) did not reflect their level of discussion. The very same children who had generated wonderful ideas during our scientists' meetings were leaving important information out when they drew and wrote in their journals. Because first graders are just learning how to become independent readers and writers, I expected them to record their observations at their own levels of writing ability. But I did not anticipate the difficulty they would have abstracting information from our discussions and investigations. Although I continued to model written entries on large chart paper for several weeks, key elements of the children's investigations continued to be omitted from their journal entries.

I should have known that some five- and six-year-olds find it difficult to organize space on a blank page. It seemed as if the science journal, in its bare state, was too open-ended for them. Blank pages are useful in many classroom situations, but these young scientists needed help remembering details, and this format forced them to be dependent on me. It was time for a change.

At our next scientists' meeting, we discussed some of the difficulties they faced when writing about their research at the lake. It was immediately apparent that the problem was largely one of format and organization of information. We brainstormed a list of the things we thought were most important to write about regardless of the experiment. Plans, materials, and labeled drawings took top priority. I brought the list home that night and designed the first of what were to be several graphic organizers on the computer. (See Figure 2.2.) Later, in the classroom, I modeled how to use it by filling out an enlarged version with my own lake plans. Then the children discussed their investigations and set out to write.

We achieved limited success with the first organizer. The children were including more information, but even though they had more organizational structure, they still weren't sure where and how to place their information on the paper. I had to rethink the organizer from the beginning. As I thought about why the children were unable to articulate their plans, I thought, how can you have a plan if you haven't first identified the question that drives the investigation? Back to the drawing board. By the next week, the class had a new organizer that better reflected how one thinks through a science problem in order to solve it. (See Figure 2.3.) The new organizer included a place for the student to share what he or she wanted to find out about the lake, a place to describe what materials were needed in order to research relevant questions, a place to draw a picture or write a sentence about the procedure to be used, and space to draw or write about the results of the investigation as well as to explain discoveries. By using this form, the students' writing improved dramatically, and they were able to enrich their journal entries with plenty of relevant details.

Figure 2.2. The First Organizer Sheet

Name: _____ Date: _____

My Trip to the Lake

1. Plan: _____

_____

_____

2. I will need: _____

_____

_____

3. Draw what you will do at the lake:

_____

4. This is what I did: _____

_____

_____

5. Draw what happened:

_____

6. Tell what happened: (I noticed . . .) _____

_____

_____

Figure 2.3. The Second Organizer Sheet

Name: _____   Date: _____

My Trip to the Lake

1. Question: _____

_____

_____

2. I will need: _____

_____

3. Draw what you will do at the lake:

_____

4. This is what I did: _____

_____

5. Draw what happened:

_____

6. Tell what happened: (I noticed . . .) _____

_____

_____

7. Why do you think this happened? _____

_____

_____

Children as Scientists: Thinking Critically

As the year progressed, the children became competent and confident scientists. I realized that it was time to step up my level of questioning and started to encourage them to look for evidence that supported their statements and theories. When they shared an observation or idea, I'd challenge them with such questions as: Why do you think this happened? What makes you think that? How can you find that out? Soon the children were looking critically not just at their own investigations and conclusions, but at the research of their peers as well. They became critical reviewers of science.

One group of children was keeping track of the birds at the lake. They were surprised by a dramatic shift in the white duck population. They shared their data with their classmates, who immediately asked why the number of ducks had decreased from five to zero. The children who had collected the data were sure that the ducks must have been eaten by the red fox. Their fellow student-scientists retorted, "How do you know?" and I asked, "What makes you think they were eaten by a fox?"

The bird experts quickly rose to the challenge, saying, "Well, we found red fox tracks by the duck prints, and there were lots of white feathers there too." (They had identified the fox tracks by using one of the field guides we regularly took with us to the lake.)

I probed a little deeper. "Why would a red fox do this?" After careful speculation, one child volunteered, "Foxes eat meat. Maybe she had to feed her babies." Another said, "Foxes go after chickens, so maybe they hunt ducks, too."

Although we had no definitive proof of what happened to the ducks, this response was indicative of an important change that had occurred in the children's thinking over the course of the year. Pat answers, which would have sufficed in the class's early days, had given way to critical thinking. The children thought through issues and assimilated information through observation, discussion, and research. They challenged one another while searching for ways to understand their environment and explain the events taking place within it.

They often worked alone during their investigations, but had learned to come together as a community to solve problems and delve into the unexplainable. They learned to respect one another's opinions, yet made suggestions that often challenged the very roots of their current theories.

Best of all, the children who were initially unfocused now found themselves in the midst of their own investigations. The children who from the start were filled with questions and who devised plans easily became models for those who were slower to articulate their own areas of interest. Over the course of a year, the wanderers became involved as they were drawn from one investigation to another, asking questions and comparing information.

All of the children had become thinkers, researchers, investigators, detectives, communicators. They learned to challenge old beliefs and devise new theories. They uncovered evidence, documented findings, and drew conclusions that sparked new questions and provided new directions of inquiry. After a year at the lake, they had become real scientists.

I, too, had changed. My confidence and comfort with inquiry-based teaching had increased. I had learned new strategies and had developed a classroom structure that allowed me to relinquish control. No longer was I tied to the narrow focus of a science guide. I learned to integrate mandated curriculum with the investigations spurred by children's questions. It was as if I was weaving a fabric, threading the children's background knowledge and emerging science concepts with the most colorful (and often unexpected) questions. The outcome was always a wonderful surprise, a design that blended theory and practice, concepts and questions, speculation and investigation. Above all, it was a true reflection of the children's understanding of the world.

CHAPTER 3

GIRLS: Girls Investigating and Researching Living Streams

MARY BETH JOHNSON

I SAT IN MY CLASSROOM, looking out at the autumn leaves swirling in the wind and wondering what I should say in the meeting that would begin in ten minutes. The principal at my new school, Beall Elementary in Montgomery County, Maryland, had asked those teachers planning after-school programs to attend a scheduling session. I was going because I wanted to repeat a project developed at my old school, Greencastle Elementary, located on the other side of our large district.

As I prepared for the meeting, my mind filled with questions. How could I build from my previous experience and adapt this program to my new teaching location? Would the new stream be big enough for the children's investigations? Would the same activities that had interested the children at Greencastle also engage the Beall students? Should attendance be limited to one age group? Who would help facilitate activities? Was there sufficient funding available to conduct a well-rounded program?

These questions were similar to ones I'd faced before, so I decided to review my earlier experiences and decisions as I considered the plans for the new program.

Year One: Getting Our Feet Wet with Stream Study

Girls and science. This was an issue that had intrigued me for years. Finally, in the summer of 1996, I decided to find an activity through which I could involve a group of girls in the processes of science. I came up with a program for ten third through fifth graders. We would investigate something local, something real, something cool for the summer and ripe with possibilities: a small stream behind our school.

I got permission from the administration and some financial support from the PTA. We came up with a catchy name, Girls Investigating and Researching Living Streams—GIRLS—and I began to put the plan in place.

Selection I wasn't sure how many girls I could accommodate in the program, but thought I could safely handle about ten or fifteen. Interested students had to complete an application and get a referral from one of their teachers.

Time Frame One week would be enough that first year, I thought. We could meet daily at the school from nine o'clock to noon, and because we had access to the school library, we'd be able to link our outdoor investigations to reading and research.

Materials and Supplies We would need special supplies and materials for the stream investigations. I had seen the equipment that the county stream teams used, but I had neither the time nor the funds to place an order. We would just have to make do with what we already had at the school, what we could purchase locally (and cheaply), and what we could make ourselves. The PTA agreed to reimburse me for a limited number of supplies, so I purchased some rubber gloves, plastic dishpans, and ice cube trays from the grocery store. I sewed pockets out of fine netting and used yardsticks for net poles. The girls brought their own waterproof boots.

Staffing It would be impossible for one person to supervise fifteen girls, so I used additional PTA funds to hire two seventh-grade helpers (school alumni) and my daughter, a college senior who had plenty of experience as an instructional aide.

Safety Safety is always an issue in science, especially when children are outdoors. I knew it would be important to leave no student unsupervised, so I was glad for the three helpers and the fact that we were able to maintain at least a 4:1 ratio of girls to staff.

Program Implementation: Management and Instructional Strategies
Since every student in the school (grades one through five) came through the science resource room, I knew that all of the girls were familiar with my teaching style and expectations. It would be smart to use the routines and classroom management techniques we'd established inside school during the academic year.

I had plenty of management strategies to fall back on. For example, in order to facilitate communication and efficiency, I planned to employ the same signals we used inside the classroom. When I wanted to get attention quickly, I used the universal sign of raising my hand. To facilitate transition, I always gave a "two-minute warning." Students responded quickly to these signals, and we wasted little time on management.

I often used the "science workshop" model established by members of the Elementary Science Integration Project (Saul 1993). Each session began with a mini-lesson—a brief instructional period designed to introduce or reinforce a specific skill or science concept. Then the students would head off in teams of five or six to various stations where they might read a prompt, write a prediction, and/or conduct a mini-investigation. They were encouraged to record their observations, using both words and labeled drawings, and to draw some conclusions from the data they had collected. Before the end of the class, we would gather for a meeting, and one person from each table would share his or her work, usually reading from a journal entry and showing illustrations. Since these routines were so well established, I thought, this would be a great way to facilitate investigations at the stream.

Testing the Waters

June arrived and it was time to "test the waters." Our homemade equipment was lined up and ready for use. The GIRLS staff were anxious to begin. Participants arrived, boots in hand.

Since everyone arrived at school at different times, we had a variety of hands-on activities set up for the early arrivals to "mess around" with. The activities were simple and familiar—magnets, sink-float, ramps and rollers—but they gave the girls something to do as they waited for the program to begin, and got them in the spirit of inquiry and investigation.

When all the girls had arrived, I went over the day's plans and held a brief mini-lesson. I taught them skills such as how to "wash rocks" to look for macroinvertebrates and reinforced how to make field notes with clearly labeled drawings. Instruction was not limited to science topics. I drew on a variety of content and process areas that related to our stream study. For example, we discussed our stream's historical significance and its importance to early Marylanders who were living in or traveling through the area. We talked about the important role streams have played in Maryland's history, powering the mills and guiding runaway slaves through the Underground Railroad. The girls were fascinated to learn that one major Underground Railroad station run by the Quakers was only five miles away from our school stream site.

After our mini-lessons, we walked to the back of the school property and began our investigations. The girls started by recording basic observations in their journals, planning to note any changes they saw in the water or land from day to day. They were expected to support their notes with detailed observations and labeled drawings and record any questions that arose while they made their observations and notes. Each girl knew that she needed to keep full, complete records in order to share data when we returned to the classroom.

Once they'd recorded their initial observations, it was time for the girls to conduct their investigation. Sometimes they'd get right in the water; other times they'd explore the shore. The week went quickly, but during that time we performed a variety of activities.

Day One On the first day we concentrated on the geography of the stream. Where did the stream come from and where was it flowing?

Day Two On the second day we looked for life in and around the stream. What types of tracks did we notice on land? Was there evidence of insect life? We caught and counted the macroinvertebrates and carefully collected, recorded, and tallied the numbers so that we could e-mail our data to the Montgomery County Stream Team. The girls worked so efficiently that day, we had time to measure water depths and temperatures in various stream locations.

Day Three Day three was devoted to the flow of the stream. Using stopwatches and ping-pong balls, we measured the water's speed in several spots. The girls noted the locations of pools and riffles in their journals.

Day Four We began day four out at the stream, but soon retreated to the science resource room in order to look through a microscope at some water samples and macroinvertebrates. The girls carefully recorded what they saw through the lens and compared their magnified drawings with those they'd made unaided. We trekked back to the stream before dismissal in order to release the "critters" back into the stream.

Day Five Our final day was devoted to completing a mural that we had been working on throughout the week. Each group of two or three girls was responsible for recording what they'd learned at one section of the stream. The completed mural accurately documented the changes in water quality and environmental condition along the area we studied. The girls painted the riffles, pools, rocks, and plants, as well as the evidence of pollution that they'd encountered while exploring. (A large rug had been dumped on the stream bank where it flows close to the road, and trash had washed off the street into the water. Downstream the water became cleaner, clearer, and less acidic, and was full of aquatic bugs and worms.)

🍃

We regularly scheduled time in the library and the lab so the girls could conduct research with a partner. They had plenty of observations and questions to share with one another and to use as the basis of their studies.

During the week, they worked in pairs and triads to investigate topics of interest: rocks, trees, grasses, birds, and bugs. Having investigated the stream firsthand, the girls had authentic reasons to turn to books and other resources. (For example, we had noticed that the water in one area of the stream appeared to be bright orange. When the "rock team" began to investigate this phenomenon, they discovered that the color was coming from a number of orange rocks. They originally attributed the odd color to pollution, but later discovered that it was more likely to be the result of iron deposits.)

The school library had just installed a computer lab with six Power Macs that the girls used for their research. My assistants were very knowledgeable about computers and were able to help the girls conduct their research on the *World Book Encyclopedia* and other CD-ROMs. I showed the girls how to use *Find-It! Science,* a child- and teacher-friendly CD-ROM database that features over 3,000 children's science trade books (available from the *Find-It!* office 410-455-2373). I picked up as many trade books as I could from my local library in order to supplement the school's resources.

Each group of girls made a formal presentation of their research. They all stood in front of their mural, wearing the GIRLS tee shirt they'd made during the week. One of the seventh-grade assistants, who attended an arts magnet school, videotaped the presentations.

GIRLS was an undeniable success. In one short week, the girls had become active and uninhibited participants in all facets of science exploration, investigation, and communication. The school benefited, too, for in the fall we aired the video on schoolwide TV, and all 650 Greencastle Elementary students shared in the girls' discoveries.

I was happy with the results of the program and hoped that I would be able to repeat it in the future. I just wasn't sure how or when it would happen.

Year Two: Expanding GIRLS

The following summer, I was presented with a new adventure. A team of three Greencastle teachers was invited to attend the Maryland Governor's Academy, a professional development program aimed at improving math and science instruction throughout the state. The academy's benefits included a series of professional development seminars, workshops, and field trips, as well as stipends, materials, and $1,000 to implement a team project.

Our team discussed many possibilities for potential projects, but after reviewing the school's MSPAP scores (statewide performance assessments given to every third-, fifth-, and eighth-grade student in the state) we noticed that no third-grade girl had scored "excellent" in science. With this indication of need, we decided to adapt GIRLS to suit the school-year schedules of three teachers and the demands of the Governor's Academy.

We decided to maintain the focus of the original program—integrating the processes of science with scientific research skills. We knew, however, that we would have to adapt many elements of the previous year's program to suit the requirements of an after-school program—and the needs of three teachers.

Funding Governor's Academy funding required that we secure matching funds from the school. We presented our ideas to the PTA and promptly received their support. These funds were augmented by grant money from the Chesapeake Bay Trust (CBT). The year before, I had enlisted the fifth-grade science-enrichment class to write a grant to CBT as an integrated science-writing activity. They conducted a preliminary needs assessment and determined that the most critical need for stream study was boots. Then, in teams of three or four students, they reviewed samples of previously written grants, and each team completed a grant application. The class voted on the one they believed best articulated the need, submitted it, and was awarded $500 to purchase boots from L. L. Bean, and pH strips and metal thermometers from a science supply company.

Student-Staff Ratio I had been the only adult involved during the first summer. This year we would have three experienced teachers. The equation seemed simple: triple the number of teachers, triple the number of students. By providing forty-five slots instead of fifteen, we would be able to open the program to fourth and fifth graders and, we hoped, include some of the girls who had participated the year before.

Although three teachers would conduct the program, we knew that, more often than not, at least one would have some other commitment during GIRLS period. So, we were grateful when two student teachers donated their after-school time. Not only were they assigned to our school for two full semesters, they were part of a special pre-service teaching program that stressed math and science. They were right in step with what we wanted to accomplish.

Scheduling Perhaps the most significant format change from year one to year two was time. Gone was the luxury of three full hours a day, five days in a row. As an after-school program GIRLS would be meeting once a month and only from 3:10 to 4:00 in the afternoon.

Time was to become our worst enemy. Each of us taught right up to the end of the school day, so we barely had time to set up for the main activity, much less manage the hands-on activities we had begun each session with the previous summer.

Hands-on, Feet-in Science

A few weeks of planning and thirty-eight girls later, we were ready to start; but it wasn't long before we discovered that this year's program would not flow as smoothly as the one I'd conducted the year before. We quickly saw that the group was too large. Not only were thirty-eight children a handful to manage effectively during such a brief session, but also seventy-six feet proved far too many to tromp through our tiny stream at one time. We were there to study the stream, not to destroy its fragile ecosystem.

Our solution was simple: we split the girls into four groups and rotated the groups through various stations. To accommodate for a lack of boots (our funds had purchased twelve pairs), two stations would be on land and two stations would be in or near the water.

Station One   At one station, eight or nine students studied the plants near the stream, looking for any birds, insects, or spiders they could draw and identify. Their task was facilitated by homemade "corn starchers." We had watched Insect Power, a Smithsonian Natural History Museum video that showed how entomologists use a similar device to locate insects in their natural habitat (available free to teachers by written request on school letterhead to O. Orkin Insect Zoo, National Museum of Natural History, Smithsonian Institution, Tenth and Constitution Ave. NW, Washington, DC 20560). As its name suggests, the corn starcher sends out a puff of cornstarch that lightly covers the spider web, making it visible without causing damage. The girls, armed with clean socks filled with cornstarch (see Figure 3.1), madly puffed the bushes, grasses, and low-lying tree branches. Once they found a web, they sketched it in their journals, along with pictures of any spiders or other insects they may have discovered.

Station Two   The second land station was located by a large old log, felled by a storm and decayed by years of wet weather, sun, and the decomposition effects of termites and millipedes. After making careful, unaided observations, the girls recorded their predictions of what they would see when they looked through a hand lens. Then they used the lens to closely examine the log and recorded their observations in their

Figure 3.1. Cornstarch Puffer Assembly

1. Take a clean white sock.

2. Fill with 1/4 to 1/2 cup cornstarch.

3. Pat (or puff) gently over bushes and rocks.

journals. We completed the exercise by taking a small piece of the decaying wood, a termite, and a millipede back to the classroom. Here we used a flex-cam and TV monitor to show a greatly enlarged view to the whole group. The girls made a third set of observations and compared them to the records of what they had seen with the naked eye and their hand lenses.

Station Three The group at station three was positioned beside the stream to measure the temperature of the water in both Celsius and Fahrenheit readings. They compared the temperatures of shallow and deep water and of still water and moving water.

Station Four The girls at the fourth station were charged with determining the speed of the stream by timing the descent of a ping-pong ball over a measured part of the stream bank. First they measured off 100 feet on the stream bank, with one girl at the start point and one at the end point. The "timer" would say, "Go!" and someone would walk the length of the track as fast as she could. This gave the girls some basis to predict how fast the balls could travel downstream. Then the timer would yell "Go!" a second time, and the girl at the top of the stream would release the ping-pong ball. When the ball reached the "catcher," who was positioned at the end point, she would yell, "Stop!" The timer then announced and recorded the time.

Using calculators, the girls figured the ball's speed by dividing the distance in feet by the time elapsed. They repeated this several times to calculate the average speed. When we returned to the classroom, they graphed and displayed their data.

🖋

Initially, we tried to rotate all the girls through all the stations each day, but we found that it was almost impossible to make meaningful observations and discoveries in ten- to twelve-minute chunks of time. So we decided to split the group—two teams went outside and two teams stayed indoors to conduct research. They switched each month: the "insiders" went out and "outsiders" stayed in.

The schedule we had originally set up was as follows:

September: Parent orientation
October: Program orientation with the girls
November: Stream observations/seasonal changes
December: Soil investigation/floods with stream table
January: Beginning student projects
February: Mixtures and compounds
March: Stream observations/research
April: Project presentations

Splitting the teams into half indoors, half outdoors forced us to add an additional stream observation in April, which pushed the project presentations to May (not an optimal time given school testing schedules).

What's My Passion?

As teachers, we sometimes get so immersed in the instructional pieces of science education, we forget that for many people, science is a passion—one they choose as their life's work. So, in addition to engaging the girls in scientific investigation and research, we felt it was important to introduce them to professional scientists who were working in the field. We wanted the children to hear stories of how these adults became interested in science as children: What sparked their curiosity? Where do they turn for answers? How is their professional research similar to the scientific investigations conducted by first-, third-, or fifth-grade scientists, or the participants in programs like GIRLS?

We were fortunate to secure some terrific guest speakers. An aerospace engineer from Lockheed Martin spoke about her own interests and encouraged the girls to consider careers in science. She patiently answered their questions and told them a great deal about women in engineering.

An amateur geologist came to talk about rocks in Maryland. He showed his personal rock collection and then took us outside to locate and identify rocks around the school. Since the fourth graders had just completed an earth materials unit in science, the girls were very interested in the geology of the stream and impressed our guest with their sophisticated questions and their knowledge.

What's My Question?

The culminating event in our yearlong program was the presentation of stream research projects. Our hope was that the stream study would spark questions, and the questions would provoke the girls to identify topics of research. We were not disappointed with the number of researchable questions they came up with. As a group, the girls brainstormed a large list of stream-related topics, then paired off as they chose topics to research. The list of topics was quite impressive: wetlands, Pfiesteria (a toxic organism associated with numerous fish kills in Maryland waters), rocks near the stream, mixtures, aquatic insects, erosion, water power, and independent stream study.

The girls used science trade books and CD-ROMs; and, thanks to the added teacher support, we were able to supplement their research with sessions on the Internet. Despite the time crunch, most teams were able to complete their research, write a report, and make posters and displays before the deadline arrived. We were pleasantly surprised by the quality and completeness of the reports, and were especially pleased that the girls' selections, research, and presentations were based solely on their own desire to learn and share. These projects were not done for grades or prizes, and none were given.

One of the more interesting research projects involved Pfiesteria, a timely and politically sensitive topic in our state. It was easy to see how the girls learned about the problem: news reports about fish kills in Maryland waters displayed ugly images of infected fish, and Governor Glendening was making television commercials assuring the public that Maryland's seafood was safe.

Two teams of girls researched Pfiesteria: what it was and how it was affecting aquatic and human life on Maryland's Eastern Shore. The girls' display was impressive. They downloaded pictures from the Internet that clearly showed the ravages of the disease on fish, and they described the impact of closing the Maryland waterways not just to fisherman but also to students, who were no longer allowed to do stream studies at their schools.

Evaluating GIRLS II

Despite the apparent success of the program in general and of the girls' projects specifically, I found numerous elements of the after-school program rather disappointing. With so many girls and so little time, it was virtually impossible for the staff to get to know each girl, let alone remember what she was researching. Although the girls wore name tags each time we met, I never fully felt a personal connection similar to what I had with the participants in the first GIRLS program.

In addition, fifty minutes was too short a time to accomplish all that we had set out to do and meeting only once a month left us vulnerable to numerous programmatic dilemmas. With a minimum of four weeks between sessions, it was difficult for lessons to build on research and investigations done the previous month, and as the school year got busier, more and more time conflicts arose between the GIRLS schedule and other after-school events. In the end, each girl got to the stream only three times during the entire program.

The whole year seemed disjointed compared to the holistic approach I was able to incorporate into the first GIRLS project. We were unable to combine history, hands-on science, research, writing, and communications all into one program.

I enjoyed working with my teaching colleagues, but I also missed planning and implementing the program on my own. I also missed the parental involvement and support that I had received in the first GIRLS program. However, although I believe that the girls in the second program missed out on a more focused and more intense personal science program, I was very proud that their projects reflected the inquiry, investigation, and research of their own questions.

The Impact of GIRLS on Girls

It is difficult to gauge the impact of the science program on the girls, mainly because they joined the program for a variety of reasons. Many girls really wanted to explore the stream. It was clear that they were already interested in science because they had stated on their applications that they liked science or wanted to be a scientist. Although working with these students was like preaching to the choir, I was glad to provide an authentic science-related activity that could reinforce their enthusiasm for science.

Other students participated simply because their friends wanted to do it. I knew these girls from the science resource room: they were usually the ones who were not comfortable with science and did not gravitate naturally toward this type of activity. These were the girls who were perhaps most affected by their participation in the program. By the end of the program, each one seemed more comfortable with nature and more willing to engage in hands-on activities. By the time they finished the program, these girls had become far more willing to participate in discussions and get involved in investigations, and they were able to make more detailed observations in their journals. They now expressed themselves, both verbally and in their written work, with greater confidence and generated a more sophisticated list of questions from their experiences. This, of course, had been a major objective of the program, and I was convinced that we'd successfully met this goal.

It was not surprising that the girls in the first year's smaller group had developed strong presentations. They had had the benefit of individual support and attention as they researched and wrote. A less anticipated payoff occurred during the second GIRLS project when the reluctant writers presented their research. These girls (often the same ones who were not on fire for science) prepared in-depth, well-organized presentations on topics of genuine interest to them. It was especially gratifying to see the work of *these* students prominently displayed in the school showcases.

Recent visits from GIRLS alumni and various messages from their parents confirm that their stream investigations have made a long-term difference. One girl even went on to become a finalist in a Toshiba science competition, a fact that her father attributes to her experiences in the science lab and the GIRLS project.

What's Next?

So now here I sit, planning my next foray into stream study. I have the experiences from two similar programs to build upon—lots of successful outcomes, and a few disappointments. Based on my dissatisfaction with last year's experience, I realize that I must begin at the beginning: rethink goals, redesign activities, readdress the reasons I want to take children outside at all. For if there is one thing I have learned, it is that one size does not fit all! I will sort through some of these ideas before I attend my meeting and make final plans for this year's stream study.

Before I plan, I'll need to decide *why I am doing this program* (besides the fact that my principal asked me to). This year, my primary goal will be to communicate to the students the importance of water; one of my secondary goals will be to use streams as the local focus of a more global concern about water. As much as I love exploring the historical development of streams in my area of the county, I realize that trying to squeeze too much into a short period of time merely dilutes the activity. Who knows? Perhaps I'll make the history of the streams Part II of this year's stream study.

When Should I Hold the Program?   Weather is obviously a major factor when scheduling outdoor investigations. It must be warm enough for us to be outside, and wet. We must also work within the confines of the school calendar and complete the program before May, when the school system schedules many tests.

How Often Should We Meet, and for How Many Weeks Should the Program Extend?   Based on past experience, I believe I need a minimum of six consecutive weeks to build a scientific community and some continuity for the participants. A six-week program will allow us to meet and formulate questions about the stream and then design investigations to answer our questions.

How Long Should Each Week's Activity Last?   I want each session to last at least an hour and a half. Now that I am back in the classroom, I will not have had contact with every student who participates in the after-school program. Unlike the participants at the Greencastle GIRLS program, who all knew my routines because they all came to my science resource room, many of the students at Beall Elementary will not be familiar with my expectations. Ninety-minute sessions will provide enough time for me to model journal writing with predictions, observations, labeled drawing, and conclusions.

Where Will We Conduct the Program?   In order to get process strategies in place, we will begin with simple indoor investigations, then move forward to outdoor learning. First we'll come together as a community of scientists, then we'll go out to do our investigations, and finally we'll return indoors to share our investigations and discoveries.

Who Will Participate?   I think this program will be limited to twelve students and, although it will no longer be a "girls only" club, at least half of the participants will be girls. It is unlikely that girls will be pushed out of the hands-on activities if their number equals or exceeds that of the boys; and having a mixed group enables boys to see that girls can do science too. (Obviously we'll need to rethink our name: GIRLS will no longer be appropriate.)

Who Will Assist Me with the Program?   For safety reasons alone, it is imperative to have at least one other adult present when taking students out to the woods and stream, so I hope to solicit one parent volunteer and one substitute. With four teams of students, each of us can manage two teams. Parent volunteers can also serve as liaisons with the PTA, telling that organization of our program successes and our needs.

What Will Our Final Product Be? As much as I loved the stream presentations and videos in the past, I found that they took up a lot of class time. I've had experience with student-written pamphlets (Johnson 1996); the student journals and research generated at the stream would lend themselves nicely to a short student-produced pamphlet that can be reproduced and stored in our library. This project can encourage student writing and artwork and will be a resource for all students in the school to use and enjoy.

🍃

The questions continue swirling in my mind. Will I miss focusing on girls, helping them to be more comfortable with science? Yes, but I'm finding that just as many boys as girls lack opportunities to explore and investigate nature. Will I miss involving large numbers of students in the program? Yes, but I won't miss feeling that the program is just window dressing for the larger problem of student science achievement. Will I miss working with colleagues and sharing the program with other educators? Absolutely, but I think I will feel more involved and invested in my own program designed for specific students. Will I miss all the activities that I have already planned and used? Yes, but I know that these new students and I will work as a team to investigate *their* questions and not just follow a rehearsed script. Together we will be a community of scientists, investigating our questions and our stream.

Annotated Bibliography

Arnosky, Jim. 1991. *Secrets of a Wildlife Watcher: A Beginner's Field Guide.* New York: Beechtree Books.
    This journal gives young readers tips about recording nature. It also has blank journal pages for their own drawings and observations.

Cherry, Lynn. 1992. *A River Ran Wild.* New York: Harcourt Brace Jovanovich.
    This narrative of the Nashua River and its pollution and cleanup gives young readers a clear picture of human impact on the environment.

Murie, Olaus J. 1974. *A Field Guide to Animal Tracks.* Boston: Houghton Mifflin.

This Peterson field guide helps identify the tracks left by animals who visit the banks of streams.

Van Cleve, Janice. 1993. *Microscopes and Magnifying Lenses.* New York: John Wiley and Sons.
This book gives some clear guidelines on how to introduce microscopes to children.

CHAPTER 4

Tasting Nature

BRENDA PICARELLO

S CIENCE WAS MY least favorite subject in high school. It seemed rigid and cold and far removed from anything that was real. It took place in a test tube or under the lens of a microscope, and it was definitely confined to the halls of the school's science wing.

It's not that I was a poor student in science—I actually excelled in the subject. In fact, every aptitude test I took during my high school years indicated that I was best suited for a career in science, but I just could not see myself working in that field. Scientists were men who "knew it all." I hadn't memorized the periodic table or the genus and species of common animals—nor did I care to. How could I possibly be a scientist if I didn't know all the facts?

When I began teaching, I didn't think about science in the same way I thought about other subjects. In science, I wanted my students to know "stuff" because I believed that the goal of science was to amass large quantities of information. Once again I faced a dilemma with science. How could I be an effective teacher of science if I didn't know all there was to know?

As a teacher of reading and language arts, I had always wanted to instill in my students a love of language and a desire to read. It never bothered me that I was teaching reading and writing without having the dictionary memorized. I understood the processes of reading and writing, so when I taught these areas of the curriculum, I knew how to foster the skills necessary for students to become successful readers and writers.

But science remained a dilemma. How could I teach it? How could I help children become scientists?

This chapter recounts how I was able to reconcile my notions of science and science teaching with my understanding of sound teaching practice and child development. I have reconstructed my journey into a rough time frame not so much to document the exact dates of events as to chronicle the evolution of my own thinking about children, teaching, and science.

The years chronicled here were an exciting time in my teaching career, during which I moved from avoiding science in the classroom to celebrating its central role in my child-centered teaching. The seeds of change were planted when I moved from first grade to pre-kindergarten. They grew slowly, soaked in the children's excitement about the world around them and nourished by my desire to provide my students with a language-rich environment. Revelations about the importance of science sprouted sporadically in a series of small trials and activities, and finally flowered during a remarkable adventure with maple trees, spiles, and buckets of sap boiling in the classroom.

August 1990

Pre-kindergarten seemed like it would be the perfect grade for me. I was returning from maternity leave and wanted to work part-time. I had just received my master's degree in reading and wanted a place to practice what I had learned about young children's reading and language acquisition. I was thrilled when I discovered that a position was available near my home.

This was perfect! I have always enjoyed teaching children who are young and enthusiastic and open and willing. I soon learned that pre-kindergarten had an added advantage I hadn't anticipated: no science! In fact, when I began the job, science wasn't mentioned in the curriculum at all.

Pre-kindergarten programs were being established in Baltimore County Public Schools as language enrichment programs. All prospective students would be screened prior to the beginning of the school year, and those children who scored lowest in language development would be accepted into the program. Language would be the program's primary focus, although math, motor, and social skills would be addressed as well.

But no science!

Early September 1990

Enter one group of enthusiastic, energetic four-year-olds. As I had with every other group of children I'd ever taught, I fell in love. I fell in love with each child individually and with the class as a whole. Although I had been looking forward to working with these students, I never realized that I would be learning from them as well. I helped the children expand their vocabularies; they introduced me to the wonders of science.

June 1991

A new interpretation of science was creeping into my classroom and consciousness. I began to realize that science was not the memorization of endless facts; rather, it was the experience of exploration and discovery. It was the wonder of the changing seasons, the delight in animal behavior, and the enjoyment of learning new things.

The American Heritage Dictionary defines science as the observation, identification, description, experimental investigation, and theoretical explanation of phenomena; methodological activity, discipline, or study; knowledge gained through experience.

Four-year-old children act out their own definitions of science. For them, science is the exploration and explanation of the world around and within them. Science is staring at a trail of ants proceeding down the sidewalk. Science is feeling the rapid beating of your heart after you have been "it" two times in a row. Science is accepting that the world is full of wonder and allowing yourself to be drawn in.

June 1992

As I looked back on my first two years of pre-kindergarten and my entry into the world of science with four-year-olds, I could see that I had taken a series of baby steps. Science hadn't just magically appeared; it had come about in increments, with investigations added slowly, and one by one. Many of the topics we had pursued began with the children's questions about the world around them. As we learned about farms, for example, the children wondered about chickens, so we hatched baby chicks in the classroom. As we studied spring, the children wondered about insects, so we watched the metamorphosis of butterflies and mealworms. Wondering about how pumpkins grew led to our planting the seeds we had saved from the pumpkins we'd carved in the fall.

My teaching was beginning to take a new direction. I still hadn't memorized the periodic table. Instead, I was beginning to see that science—more specifically, children's natural curiosity—was the most natural way to enhance language while supporting and enriching all other curricular areas.

When children begin to use oral language, they begin to question. "Why?" If you know any speaking child, you've heard this question—repeatedly. Now, in our classroom, questions were becoming more common and less feared, a springboard for the direction of our studies. The children reveled in this new learning. Their sense of wonder in the world grew, and I began to see science in our classroom as a continuous experience, not as a series of isolated experiments or encounters. Although I never would have predicted it, I was actually looking forward to continuing these science adventures in my classroom the next year.

September 1992

In September 1992 I transferred to a school near my home. Although Edmondson Heights was located just a few miles outside of the Baltimore city line, there were plenty of opportunities for outdoor exploration. We had grass, weeds, and trees; plenty of insects; and always clouds—that just might look like spilt milk.

We began using outdoor time as an opportunity for observation and exploration, not just for playground time. Autumn meant more to us when we closely observed the changes in our schoolyard. We no longer walked through the school to get to the bus, but went out our classroom door and followed whatever path our curiosity led us to—past walnut and oak trees where autumn leaves, nuts, and acorns fell to the ground all around us.

June 1993

By the end of the school year, I was thinking a lot about the connections between language (the established focus of our pre-kindergarten curriculum) and science (the emerging focus of our pre-kindergarten activity). As young learners, four-year-olds often don't—because they can't yet—make the same kind of connections that older children make. They are just starting down the path of wonder and inquiry, just beginning their own adventures. These adventures give them a reason for speaking and a need to write, record, and share.

Gradually, I was discovering how easily I could link these concepts. Whether we were hatching baby chicks, exploring items that sink and float, or taking part in our weekly cooking session, the children were anxious to talk about their observations and discoveries, and I had plenty of their words and sentences to record and display around the room.

February 1994

In early 1994 a new adventure was on the horizon. It arrived in the form of questions from my own sons, Bryan and Jeffrey.

One cold February morning, the boys and I took a trip up to Oregon Ridge Nature Center, a Baltimore County park facility several miles north of the city. Bundled in warm clothing, we trekked through the snow and watched the naturalists tap maple trees. We saw how the sap was collected before we walked back to the sugar house, where we watched them boil down the sap to make syrup. The experience was wonderful, but as we began to drive home I considered it was over.

I should have known that with children nothing is ever quite over. Children don't set boundaries for learning or compartmentalize experiences the way adults do.

After a few moments of silence, a small voice rose from the back seat. "Mom, those were maple trees, right?"

"Yes."

"And the trees in our backyard are maple trees, right?"

I could see where this was going and I didn't like it. "Yes," I responded, more warily this time.

"Can we tap our trees when we get home?"

I felt that sinking feeling I get when I know I can't give my children all they want. I'm not a naturalist. I didn't have the special equipment naturalists have. I certainly didn't know anything about tapping trees. I knew what my answer must be.

"Yes."

For the remainder of the ride home I worried endlessly. How would we make this work? Where would we find the appropriate equipment? Would we kill the trees?

I also started to dream.

Because I both lived and taught in the same neighborhood, a community of about 1,200 row homes, I was very familiar with the area. The builder had planted a large number of maple trees, they grew fast and provided lots of shade. I thought, if I can do this with my family, why couldn't I tap maple trees with my students? What an authentic way to explore science!

I never would have considered such an undertaking just a year or two earlier. I would have focused on the reasons why I could not do this rather than look for ways to make it possible. But now I was committed. I would make this happen.

I had to work fast. Maple trees are tapped at the end of the winter season when daytime temperatures rise above freezing and nighttime temperatures drop below. We were rapidly approaching that time in Maryland.

I needed to gather materials and get my principal's permission if we were going to try maple sugaring this year. Luckily, my principal was supportive of the idea and gave her permission. I sent letters and permission slips home with my students.

The community response was immediate and positive. All of the parents gave permission for the walk off school grounds, and four families said that they had trees we could tap. Interestingly, not all of these trees grew in my students' yards. One was in a grandparent's yard; another was in a neighbor's.

Now all I had to do was collect materials and practice on my own trees at home.

I hadn't thought of trying to tap trees myself as I watched the naturalists at Oregon Ridge Nature Center. I was merely an interested observer. But now that I was going to lead this activity myself, I needed more—lots more—information. The center naturalists were more than willing to help me get started, explaining procedures and giving me a list of useful books and supplies.

Maple trees, I learned, are tapped by drilling a two-and-a-half-inch hole, inserting an instrument called a spile (a hollow metal spout that keeps the sap from dripping down the side of the tree), and attaching a metal bucket to the spile to collect the sap. I didn't have a spile or a metal bucket, and I certainly had no experience using them in this way.

In the past, worries about specialized equipment kept me from feeling comfortable about teaching science. Science simply required too many objects that I had no experience with. But now I was finding that asking for help and using available resources could lighten my load.

Since I needed a spile in a hurry and didn't know where I could get one, I delegated responsibility for acquiring a spile to my husband, Mike. I gave him the specifications, and he disappeared into that area of the basement where he keeps all his tools. I knew how enthusiastically he collects things, and I was sure he would have what I needed.

After several minutes in the basement, he returned with the perfect object. It was thin and hollow and could be easily inserted into a hole drilled in a tree—just like the naturalists did. It was also long enough to direct the flow of sap. But I was not convinced it would work. Mike had simply removed the caps and ink cartridge from a disposable pen. This surely wasn't the tool that the naturalists had used!

Then I thought about how spiles had probably been developed. People must have decided that they no longer wanted the sap to run down the side of the tree, so they devised a tool, out of the materials they had at hand, that would make sap collection more efficient. This is just what Mike had done. I decided to give his spile a try.

March 1994

By the time we were ready to set out for the trees in early March, I had adapted a number of standard tapping procedures. Some procedures and materials were changed because of the needs of my students, who were, after all, small children; others were adapted simply because they were better suited to our situation—and our budget.

The naturalists at Oregon Ridge had used manual hand drills to make their holes. I wasn't sure that the children would have the strength to use such a drill, so I decided to pack both a manual and an electric drill. Also, rather than using a metal bucket to collect the sap, we attached rubber tubing to the end of our homemade spile and ran the tubing into a small hole in the side of a milk jug on the ground. Milk jugs were more readily available than metal buckets, and the tops can be sealed to keep falling leaves and other debris out of the sap.

I kept the activity that first year, both at home and in school, very open-ended. I wasn't sure how successful our project would be, but I was willing to give it a try. I knew that we would learn some valuable lessons whether or not we were able to collect the sap and boil it down into syrup.

In the end, we were successful! We tapped the trees, collected sap, and made our own syrup. Along the way, we were driven to question, research, read, and learn—a lot.

The experience of tapping maple trees integrated all curricular areas. We wrote language experience stories about our walks. We recorded our procedures in a journal. We consulted books for more information about trees. We measured and graphed how much sap we collected from each tree. And we learned more about the life of people who live in the areas where trees are tapped commercially.

The children's language development (always our primary goal) was amazing. This strange process of collecting "stuff that looks like water" from trees in their neighbors' yards and then turning it into something they could pour on their waffles and eat was exciting. The children spoke repeatedly and with purpose. Inspired to tell their parents, siblings, schoolmates—almost anyone who would listen—they learned and used both basic words and terminology specific to tapping trees. Their desire to relay their excitement pushed them to incorporate a variety of words and phrases and add descriptive details to their stories. Explaining the procedures we'd followed made them think about sequencing.

I was learning, too—discovering that I didn't need to know it all. There was no way I could. Many scientists spend their entire professional careers focused on one narrow area of research, so why should or could I know everything? I was increasingly comfortable with the notion that I could learn along with the children.

Tapping maple trees and making maple syrup was to become a yearly, eagerly anticipated event. People who had seen our group walking through the neighborhood called or sent messages asking what we were doing or if their tree could be tapped. Parents whose schedules were often too busy to allow them to visit school took time off from work to accompany us on our trips through the neighborhood. Those who were unable to visit during the day checked out the sites in the evening with their children.

September 1994

As I began my long-range plans for the new school year, I reviewed the previous year's maple syrup experience and thought about how I could expand it, make it more inclusive.

I'd been thinking a lot about another teacher in the school, Todd Loht. Mr. Loht didn't realize he was on my mind, but he'd been lodged there since the previous winter, when his fourth graders stopped my pre-kindergartners as they were on their way back from tapping trees. The older students asked where we had been and what was in the milk jugs that we were carrying. As my students explained our project, I started thinking. What would happen if we included the fourth-grade students next year? Would this activity be something both classes would benefit from? Would such a large group be manageable?

I asked Todd if he was interested. Yes, he said, he'd give it a try. Now we needed to find ways to ensure that the activity was not just fun, but also meaningful for both groups of students. We needed to make it a vehicle for learning that supported the curriculum we were both charged with teaching.

Finding curricular connections was easy. Tapping maple trees fit nicely with the pre-kindergarten study of seasons. It also tied in with the fourth-grade study of plants.

Time was a problem. Some of the yards we would be visiting were quite a distance from school. Just walking back and forth would take up much of the period, but we also needed time to record observations, identify the trees, and then tap them to collect the syrup. Todd wanted time for his students to write in their journals while on site, and we both needed time once we returned to school. Follow-up discussion and reflection were critical, for they would enable the children to make meaning of the events of each day.

Time had not been as much of a problem when I was scheduling pre-kindergartners within our long two-and-a-half-hour block, but Todd needed to work his schedule around lunch, special activities, chorus, and instrumental music. There was no way we could get everything in for every child. We decided that our best solution was to conduct some portions of the activity together, but separate the groups for grade-specific instruction and discussion.

We hoped that the joint activity would reciprocally benefit both groups of students. I expected that my pre-kindergarten students would get more involved simply because they would benefit from one-on-one direction from the older students. Todd hoped that his fourth-grade students would gain a sense of responsibility as they aided the younger children.

October–November 1994

As the fall progressed, the four-year-olds observed and documented the natural world and spent extra time learning how to identify trees. Maples, dogwoods, and oaks were the most common trees in our neighborhood, and it wasn't long before the children could identify them by the shape and color of their leaves. In anticipation of our upcoming tree tapping, we searched out maple trees close to the school.

February 1995

Finally, February arrived. It was time to tap the maple trees in our neighborhood. But before we could go, we needed to make sure that we'd be tapping the right trees. My students were convinced they would be able to identify the maples—they had found it easy to do in the fall.

Although we'd been documenting the many changes of the seasons, when we approached the trees in early February the children were stunned to discover that there were no leaves they could use to identify the maples! We stood beneath the trees and pondered our dilemma. How would we ever know which trees to tap?

But young children faced with obstacles always seem to find a way of climbing over them. One child suggested that we look at the bark to differentiate tree types. Others suggested size, shape, branches, or location. Not all of the suggestions were viable ones, but the children knew that if they thought about it they would be able to determine some way to tell which trees were maples.

At this point I decided to introduce the idea of opposite and alternating leaf buds on branches as a means of tree identification. Although a few children used the proper (adult) terminology, others said that either branches had leaf buds that were "partners" or leaf buds that "took turns." We referred to our trusty field guides and soon were able to identify the leafless maples by their opposite leaf buds and bud clusters at the ends of their branches. Even though the four-year-olds could not read the reference books, they became very adept at using the guides to identify trees by noting specific characteristics in the illustrations.

Finally, in the third week of February, the big day arrived. Fourth graders descended from the second floor to pair up with their four-year-old partners. Todd had told his students that each of them would be responsible for one four-year-old, and that they should be prepared that not all of the younger ones would follow directions well. It was exciting to see how seriously the fourth graders took their responsibility. And it was amusing to see how exasperated they became when four-year-olds exhibited some of the same behavior they did with their teachers ("Mr. Loht, I've already told him five times and he still won't listen!").

After a brief walk ("How much longer? I'm tired"), we arrived at the first yard. We asked the children to identify which tree we would tap. After the pre-kindergartners checked the branches and leaf buds, they located the maple.

We selected an easily accessible spot on the trunk, and the children took turns drilling the two-and-a-half-inch hole (I was glad that I'd brought the electric drill as a back-up). Then we inserted the empty pen tube and ran rubber tubing from our spile to a milk jug we had placed on the ground by the tree.

The sap began to run as soon as we drilled the hole. Some children were excited by its immediate appearance. Others were disappointed that it looked like water. They were sure we'd made some mistake until they took a taste. Although some children were disgusted with the thought of eating something from a tree, several brave souls noted the sap's slight sweetness. Others said it tasted like water.

We continued our trek through the neighborhood, tapping the designated trees and leaving behind a supply of empty milk jugs so that each homeowner could continue to collect and save the sap for us. Each jug was marked with a number that identified which yard, and tree, the sap came from. Then we headed back to the classroom.

Four-year-olds and fourth graders gathered together in the pre-kindergarten classroom. They needed time to reflect on and discuss this unique experience. They reviewed the events of our trip and asked many questions. I recorded some of their comments:

Sap came out of the tree.
It looked like water.
It looked like sap.
When it rains the sap will come down from the tree and into the bucket.
How much will we get?
How does it work?
Does the size of the tree mean how much sap we get?
What happens next?

After our discussion, the children reconnected with their partners to write a story about their experience. It was wonderful to watch how well the four-year-old children worked with their older colleagues. Todd had designed a graphic organizer to help the older children elicit stories from the younger ones (Figure 4.1). The fourth graders were forced to think about what had occurred as they interviewed the younger children and encouraged them to recall and sequence the steps we followed. The four-year-olds responded well to the individual attention they so rarely received in a classroom setting.

Because leaving the school grounds required special permission, we made only two trips to our tapping sites. Many of the children monitored progress at the trees after school hours and reported back to the class. They checked the sites on their way to and from school or took neigh-

---

Figure 4.1. Todd's Organizer

Maple Tree Sugaring

Here are some ideas for writing a story with your partner.

Write the steps in order for tapping maple trees.

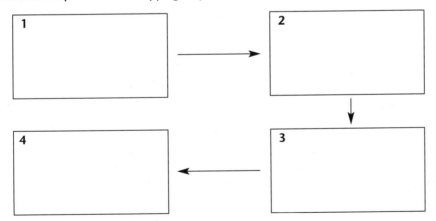

What did you enjoy?

What questions do you have about the experience?

Was there anything you did not like?

Now, write a story with your partner using the above information.

borhood walks with their parents in the evenings. One day, a parent came rushing in after school to ask for the address of a particular tree. She knew of it only by site number and wanted to stop by with her child.

We never could have anticipated the mystery we would have to solve when we made our trip to collect the sap. Although most of the trees we had tapped were of similar size, our rate of collection was very uneven. We collected nine-and-a-half gallons of sap from one tree and none at all from another. A tree that produced less than half a gallon this year had produced four-and-a-half gallons the previous year. What happened?

The children had to become scientists as they attempted to solve the mystery. They were filled with questions and theories. They recorded the weather conditions and the relative position of the sun, and noted whether the spile was hammered into the sunny side or the shady side of the tree. They measured the diameter of the trees and took note of the fact that some trees had recently been pruned.

We gathered our clues and returned to school with our jugs full of sap. We assembled on the rug so the children could share their observations.

> It looks like maple sap.
> There is sugar in it.
> There is ice in the sap.
> It looks like apple juice and water.
> Did the temperature make a difference?
> If the tree is in the sun will it have more sap?
> That really isn't sap, it's just water.
> How come Miss Lori's tree only had a little bit?
> Wow! Nine-and-a-half gallons—that's a lot!

I dutifully recorded every comment and question on pieces of chart paper and hung them on the wall before sending the children off in partners to graph the amount of sap we had collected. Todd and I had generated a graphic organizer on the computer containing illustrations of milk jugs that the children could cut out and paste on a simple graph (Figure 4.2), each jug representing one gallon of sap. This activity fit neatly with both classes' curriculum: the pre-kindergartners were working on counting and constructing small sets, while the fourth-grade students were learning about graphs.

As soon as we saw the results from our highest-yielding tree, of course, Todd and I realized the graphs weren't going to work. Nothing in my limited experience had prepared me for a single tree producing nine-and-a-half gallons of sap in such a short period of time. The form we developed had enough space to glue on a maximum of six jugs. There was no way to squeeze nine or ten jugs onto the graph.

Figure 4.2. Creating a Graph

Graph the amount of sap drawn from each tree. Be sure to include all the necessary parts of a graph.

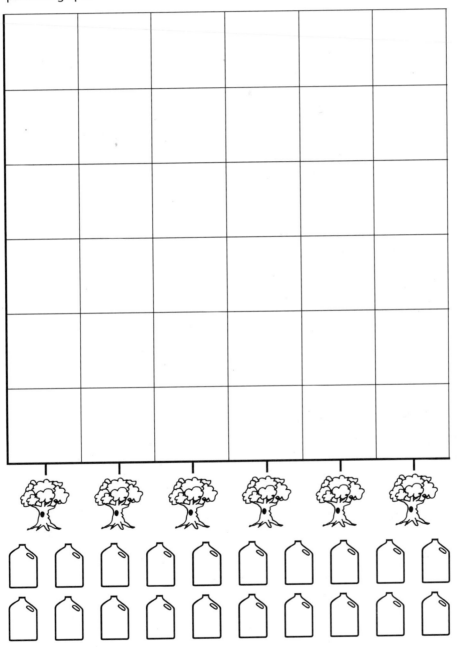

We had to decide quickly what to do. Because we had created the form on the computer, we knew it would be easy to modify it before we gave it to the children. In the end, we decided to leave the form as it was and see what solutions the children would come up with.

We weren't disappointed. Some partners decided to have each jug represent two gallons of sap. Others chose to glue two jugs onto each square. A few simply continued the column up the page as if there were additional squares. In the end, all the children came up with a meaningful and appropriate solution.

March 1995

Next came the tasty part—boiling the sap down into syrup. Todd and I divided the sap between us and set up pots and hot plates in our respective classrooms. We established a means for recording cooking procedures and the children's observations because we wanted to compare notes after we'd made our syrup. I used large chart paper and helped the pre-kindergartners record their information, and we set up times during the day when the children could examine the boiling sap. An adult was stationed nearby, both for safety and to record the children's comments on the chart.

March 5, 1995:

We started cooking the sap.
The sap looked like water.
It's looking like bubbles.
It's bubbling.
Under the bubbles it's looking browner.
It's looking like it has white glasses.
It smells delicious.
We added more sap.
It's really big because there's more sap.
It's fuller.

March 6, 1995:

We filled the pot.
I smell it.
It smells like cake.
It smells like peanut butter and jelly.
It smells like it's supposed to—sap.
I saw bubbles.
It looks green.

It looks yellow.
It looks like syrup.

Like everything else in teaching, we had to adapt—in this case, we needed to adjust the process of boiling the sap. We didn't have a pot large enough for all the sap to boil at one time, so we poured enough sap into our pots to fill them, then boiled it throughout the day, adding more sap from the jugs as the level in the pots became low. We refrigerated the remaining sap each night. This procedure doesn't yield the highest-quality syrup, but it would suffice for our purposes.

Each year we learn something new about the sap-to-syrup process. In 1995 both classes learned hard lessons about how quickly the sap becomes syrup after several long days of boiling.

It was almost time to remove the syrup from the hot plate in the pre-kindergarten classroom. The syrup was brown and very obviously beginning to thicken. Suddenly, a child became ill and needed my undivided attention. By the time I had rushed to the health room and back, the syrup had burned. Although I would have liked to forget the incident, we had to record our observations so that we could pass our hard-learned lessons along to subsequent classes.

The sap burned.
It looked liked sticky buns.
It looked like chocolate.
It had bubbles.
It looked like a brown cookie.
It looked brown.

Meanwhile the fourth-grade class was having its own problems. They had to leave for a special at the same critical point that our cooking had gone awry. In the few short minutes it took for Todd to walk his students across the hall, the fourth grade's syrup burned as well.

First we panicked. Then we started over. The next day we salvaged what was left of the sap and proceeded to make syrup again, this time being much more careful to stand by during those final, critical minutes.

By mid-March we had syrup (although less than we'd originally hoped for). Now it was time to taste it. But first, I brought in a number of different kinds of syrup so that the children could compare their syrup with other types. I hung graphs on the wall so that they could indicate their preferences.

I have never been good at picking bests, so I did not require the children to select one favorite. Instead, I asked them to indicate whether or not they liked each type of syrup. The children tasted our homemade syrup, store-bought maple syrup, and store-bought pancake syrup (containing no real maple). Many of them were surprised that the flavor of real maple syrup, whether store-bought or homemade, was different from what they had expected.

Every Friday in pre-kindergarten we cook our own snack, so we invited the fourth grade to join us for waffles and syrup. Although many children had indicated that they liked the maple syrup, pancake syrup was by far the most eaten type that day.

June 1995

I enjoyed collaborating with another teacher and class. Originally, Todd and I had been concerned about the logistics: safety, curricular links, and time constraints. In retrospect we were pleased at just how child-centered the experience had been. Students in both classes were able to start with the organization and structure of our planned activity and branch off into new and interesting directions.

Some children wanted more information about tree classification and turned to books and field guides for their answers. Others wanted to learn more about the maple-syrup-making process. They wrote letters outside of their language arts time to get more information from experts. Some children wanted to find out what other types of syrup were available and conducted a search of local grocery stores. Through our planned activity, all of the children were given a springboard for investigation and allowed to find solutions to their own areas of interest.

Some of our questions were never answered that year. We still don't know exactly how tree size and quantity of syrup are related. We didn't see any link between the recent trimming of one of the trees and the amount of sap collected. We don't know how the relative position of the sun affects sap production. Perhaps the children who tapped maple trees that year will be inspired to try again so they can answer these—or a whole new set of questions.

🍂

I continued to tap maple trees with students at Edmondson Heights for several years, sometimes with four-year-olds only, sometimes in collaboration with older students. Each year the experience was fresh and exciting. New groups of students with new needs and new interests provoked new experiences and new questions. But as I revisit the old adventures and look forward to new ones, I cannot help noting my own rich and rewarding, and continually evolving, definitions of science and think back fondly to a group of four-year-olds who invited me to join their exploration of the world.

CHAPTER 5

It Started with a Stream

KAREN SHRAKE

I T IS A COLD SATURDAY in November, and I should be curled up in a cozy chair reading—or doing anything indoors, even vacuuming. Instead, my partner, Mike Zimmerman, and I are tromping in hip boots along a path in the woods with several hearty fourth graders and their dedicated parents and siblings. Our destination is a riffle in the Paint Branch, a stream in Montgomery County, Maryland. Our school, Burtonsville Elementary, monitors the quality of the stream through biological and chemical testing. In a few moments we will carefully enter the stream, set up seines, and plunge our hands into the numbing water to rub critters off of submerged rocks into the waiting nets.

As the first children cross over the wooden bridge toward our site, I hear their excited voices.

"Hey, there's a dead fish on the bridge! How did it get here?"

"I bet the stream rose above the bridge and left the fish."

"Look at the plants over here! They're lying flat!"

"It looks like the stream overflowed its banks and bent the grass—it's all facing downstream."

I marvel at the children's alert observations, questions, and informal hypothesizing and remember why I am braving the cold, damp weather.

We all peer into the stream. It's higher than normal, definitely running faster than usual, but still safe to monitor. We wonder—will we find the stream teeming with life? Is this the time of year when insect larvae still live underwater? How did the storm affect stream life? Have any pollutants entered the stream through the runoff? What about macroinvertebrates other than insect larvae—are they hunkering down for the winter?

I love the children's natural curiosity. They always ask so many questions about so many things, but their questions on this November day are focused and purposeful, based on a growing understanding of the stream life they are encountering on a regular basis. How did the students come to this level of awareness in such a short time?

In the Beginning

This story actually originates not with the children but with me—my own introduction to a stream team project and the distance I've traveled in a lifelong quest for learning more about the world in which I live. So along with asking how my students arrived at this point, I must ask how I got to this stage in my growth as a teacher.

A large part of my personal and professional development has been nurtured through the collegiality of many dedicated teachers and the affirmation I have received from them. As I consider my colleagues, my "stream team buddies," I think of words that describe their wonderful qualities: curious, enthusiastic, fun-loving, dedicated, innovative, hard-working, creative, earnest.

Sandi Geddes, Joanne Kress, Patrick Stevens, and I are fourth-grade teachers from different schools in a very large, county-based school district within the Chesapeake Bay watershed. When we met at an elementary science training several summers ago, we quickly forged a bond and soon began looking forward to seeing one another at the science lead teacher meetings. Each time we got together, we compared notes about what we had added to, deleted from, and integrated into our science units. We yearned to work with one another and were waiting for the right opportunity to come along. It finally arrived in the form of a unique environmental studies project.

One fourth-grade unit, the National Science Resource Center's Ecosystems unit, fit perfectly with our social studies unit on the Chesapeake Bay. The kit included materials and directions for students to build ecocolumns—terrariums and aquariums made from two-liter bottles. These small enclosed systems provide living models through which children can observe the interactions and interdependence of plants and animals. By adding new elements to their ecocolumns, students can see and record the effects of pollutants on their bottled environments.

While working with the ecocolumns, the students and I discussed the advantages and disadvantages of using models to study large systems. On the positive side, ecocolumns gave us an "up close and personal" look at how land and water ecosystems are interrelated. We all agreed that testing and observing pollutants in model ecosystems was far safer than actually adding pollutants to real-world ecosystems.

However, there was a downside to using these small models to learn about the larger world. There was very little biodiversity in our bottled environments—just crickets and isopods living among three plant varieties in the terrariums, and fish and snails living among three aquatic plant types in the aquariums.

We needed to get outside.

A Whole New World

About this time, my colleagues and I discovered that fellow science lead teacher Kathryn Show was doing stream studies with her elementary students. She asked if we were interested in learning more about her program. We certainly were! But how would we get started? How could we learn enough about streams ourselves? What equipment would we need, and how would we pay for it?

Kathryn explained how she wrote a Chesapeake Bay Trust grant proposal. (The Chesapeake Bay Trust, an organization dedicated to preserving the Chesapeake Bay, receives donations from Maryland taxpayers and funds projects that help preserve the Bay.) We in turn wrote grant proposals of our own to fund the supplies we needed. In my first proposal, I requested funds for hip boots, seines, and chemical test kits. My school provided matching funds for field guides and special fiber-optic microscopes that could withstand our fourth graders' rigorous handling when taken to the stream.

We turned to the Montgomery County Department of Environmental Protection (DEP) and the Izaak Walton League for training in water quality monitoring protocol. I also attended an on-site training session sponsored by the Audubon Society. Before setting off for the stream, we sat together, with experts helping novices, as we familiarized ourselves with the stream insect larvae and crustaceans, otherwise known as macroinvertebrates, or simply bugs. My head was spinning, and a fear of inadequacy began to trickle through my system—a dull, aching self-doubt. How was I going to memorize two dozen strange-looking creatures? How could I teach this to my students when I was overwhelmed? (Actually, this was a valuable experience for me as a teacher. It put me in a student's place, and reminded me of those times when one can feel overwhelmed by information overload.)

Okay, I said to myself, a stonefly larva has two tails and a mayfly larva has three, except for one kind that has two. But don't worry, you can tell it apart from a stonefly because of its gills. Gills? What do bug gills look like? How can I remember which bugs are pollution sensitive and which are pollution tolerant? There is that third category in the middle—the *somewhat* pollution tolerant. Don't forget that there are right-opening snails and left-opening snails.

This was much more than I ever wanted to know about snails. I was definitely not ready to go outside. But out we went, and the Audubon people were terrific. We broke up into small, guided groups, each going to a different riffle in the stream. We set up seines. We rubbed rocks and massaged the streambed. The sights and sounds were invigorating—gurgling water, a gentle wind in the newly budding trees, and shouts of excitement from my fellow participants. As I pulled up my sleeves and dipped my hands in the water, I knew this was what both my students and I needed to make the connection from the classroom to the real world.

We pulled our seines out of the water, set them on the bank, and examined our catch. Our guide pointed out different body parts—antennae, legs, tails—that helped identify the critters. This wasn't so hard. True, some were a challenge to identify, but we did the best we could using the printed pictures and descriptions we had carried with us. (The Save Our Streams people from the Izaak Walton League provided an excellent identification chart.) We tallied the macroinvertebrates in each category and found the stream to be in good condition. (A wide diversity of plants and animals indicates a healthy stream.)

My apprehension began to subside. I had been able to conduct a stream study my first time out, and I imagined that my students, too, would be able to participate fully in our own stream studies. I could provide them with training and laminated copies of the bug chart they'd need to make the necessary identifications.

I also knew that I could rely on the children's natural curiosity and my own developing interest in both the study of streams and the pedagogical issues related to inquiry-based teaching. Just as the teaching in my classroom is driven by children's questions, I knew that this stream study project would be guided by my own questions about the stream and its connection to the immediate neighborhood, macroinvertebrates, student learning, and the role of science in the classroom.

The beauty of inquiry science (or inquiry anything, for that matter) in a cohesive classroom community is that individuals may pursue unique interests while conferring with others. Sometimes, when students share their questions with their classmates, they find that their peers have similar questions. Other times, one classmate's question can serve as a springboard for another's inquiry. The children are catalysts for each other's questions and learning. If children are not allowed to pursue their questions but instead must seek a predetermined answer to a teacher's question, where is the motivation?

As a teacher, observing and participating in the children's quest for answers are very stimulating for me. I feel the same exhilaration when I network with my colleagues. In a way, the two situations are like parallel universes: I'm going through the same experiences outside the classroom that my students are going through inside. Sharing that process brings me closer to my students.

Same Questions, Many Solutions

I was intrigued to find that, as we set up stream teams at our respective schools, my friends and I were asking many of the same questions: How can I manage a class of 28 to 30 students at the stream? I can't have them all in the stream at the same time, but if I divide them into small groups, will I find enough riffles to keep them within my sight? How can I spread myself thin enough to oversee the identification at each net? How do I go about training parent volunteers?

Although we teach in the same county, our school situations are quite different, and we set up our stream monitoring in various ways. Sandi monitors Little Falls Stream, a small, four- to five-foot-wide neighborhood runoff stream adjacent to the school. She sends home one permission slip per student for the entire year, arranging for the children to leave the school property several times a year to walk to the source of the stream and monitor it. She hires a substitute, recruits parents, and takes a third of her class at a time for a fifty-minute directed lesson. Students are divided into two small groups, each monitoring its own riffle. Because of the small amount of biodiversity and the type of macroinvertebrates they find, they consider themselves lucky if they get a "fair" reading. They often bring the bugs back to the classroom for further examination (Sandi later returns them to the stream).

Joanne's stream has no name, is not much wider than three feet, and meanders through the neighborhood, feeding into Little Seneca Lake. It's within a half-hour walk of the school. With at least three parent volunteers, she takes her whole class to the stream while one parent drives the equipment. Dividing her class into three groups, she stations each group with a parent at a different site, all within her sight. Each group is then divided in half. While one half-group is in the stream, the other half surveys the bank for shade, composition (trees, shrubs, grass, bare soil, rocks), and signs of erosion, and performs chemical tests. When the groups are finished with their tasks, they switch places, so there will be two readings from each site. Near the end of the visit, the whole class meets at a bridge, shares critters they have found, and examines them with microscopes before returning them to the water.

Patrick's stream, the Dry Seneca Creek, flows through woods and farmland. Like Sandi, he hires a substitute. Leaving two reading groups with the sub, he takes two groups at a time outside with him. Sometimes they walk; other times, if there are enough volunteers, parents drive the students to the sites. They usually monitor a riffle upstream from a waste treatment plant and then a riffle just downstream from the plant. They often find that the stream is healthier just below the plant.

My situation was different. There is a stream directly behind my school, but it was too dangerous to monitor. Years of unchecked erosion created by parking lot runoff has carved steep, crumbling banks that are twenty- to thirty-foot cliffs. (Thank goodness a fence separates the school playground from this danger!) So, despite the proximity of this stream to our school, I had to find a different one to monitor.

The Paint Branch, for which our local high school is named, is the next nearest stream. Whereas my stream buddies could walk to their water, I had to arrange bus transportation to ours. The site is only a ten-minute ride from our school, but it is far enough away to prevent our being able to hike to it with all our equipment.

There were other restrictions, too. We discovered that the Paint Branch was the only stream in Montgomery County in which the brown trout spawned naturally. To avoid disturbing the redds—the fish egg deposits—and possibly destroying hundreds of trout eggs, we could not enter the stream between late November and late April. We therefore limited our monitoring to fall and late spring and took no winter readings. If we had not registered with DEP, we may have, in our ignorance, hurt a stream that we were trying to help.

Connection to Others

Timing is everything. Around the time we were taking our first dips in the stream, our school system was starting an intranet system called "First Class" for which teachers were given e-mail accounts. "Wouldn't it be neat," Joanne thought, "if our students could send e-mail to each other, describing their trips to the stream and sharing data?"

The four of us met at a restaurant to set up "key pal" (keyboard pen pal) teams for our students. The first year, we grouped students in what we thought would be compatible teams, but since then Patrick has developed a survey for students to complete (see Figure 5.1). If a student who loved writing in school and playing outside during her free time wanted to be in a group of all girls, she would receive a score of 1-4-1 to coincide with the numbers in the survey. Then, when the time came for us to put the key pal teams together, we would look for similar 1-4-1 combinations from each school and placed these students on the same team. Ultimately, we would have around 24 key pal teams.

Figure 5.1. Key Pal Survey

Name: _____   Score: _____

Circle the phrase that best completes the sentence.

A. I want to be in a team of…
   1. all girls.
   2. all boys.
   3. half girls and half boys.

B. My favorite subject is…
   1. math.
   2. reading.
   3. science.
   4. writing.

C. I like to spend my free time…
   1. playing outside.
   2. playing computer games.
   3. reading or writing.

Each of my students had three key pals, one from each of the other three classes. They could each send a single letter to their key pals in the other three schools and receive three letters in return. What could be easier? As it turned out, because some classrooms only had access to one or two computers, practically anything would be easier, even churning out three grueling, handwritten letters per student. Actually, this task was easier for me than it was for my colleagues. My school was newly renovated and had a new Macintosh computer lab, so all of my students had easy access to computers. My buddies had no such luxury, but they managed to come up with creative ways to get almost thirty students onto one or two Macs to write their letters. (An example of a letter one of my students wrote to her key pals is shown in Figure 5.2.)

Sandi and Patrick also thought it would be a good idea to get our students together. The children were getting to know their key pals through letters, but a face-to-face meeting would make their communication more personal. Patrick came up with the idea of a Stream Fest, an environmental festival in which students from all four classes would meet, participate in various outdoor activities, and monitor a stream.

We all knew what this meant! The four of us would simply have to meet for dinner to hammer out the details. By the time we left the

---

Figure 5.2. Letter to Key Pals

Dear Katie, Gina, and Amy,

On Saturday, we went to our stream. We found 8 caddisflies,* 0 mayfly, 3 dobson-flies, 3 crayfish, 1 flyfish, 6 crane flies, and 5 aquatic worms. It was a fair rating, but we think the Paint Branch is really in good condition because we got a good dissolved oxygen reading and the water was 52 degrees Fahrenheit.

We are learning about electric circuits in science class now. We just tested conductors and insulators. What are you guys doing in science?

For Literature Study Groups, we are reading *A Jar of Dreams*. What are you reading?

Your key pal,

Jenny

P.S. Write back soon. See you at the next Stream Fest.

* We actually found larva and nymphs, not the actual adult flies.

---

restaurant, we had drawn up plans; soon afterward, we set a date. We were ready to roll.

The Stream Fest

On the day of the festival, the weather was on our side—the late October air was crisp, the sky a dazzling blue. More than a hundred children, twelve parent chaperones, a handful of high school environmental club members, and volunteers to run the stations were raring to go. With eyes wide open, fingers crossed, and hearts pounding, we embarked on our adventure.

We had divided the students into six "color groups" of about sixteen children. By taking our key pal roster and designating teams one through four to be the orange group, teams five through eight to be the pink group, and so on, the children would be in groups with their key pals, and the groups would be evenly filled with students from all four schools. These groupings allowed us to assign and rotate groups to activities throughout the day.

Small groups of key pals from different schools collaborated on monitoring the stream. One group identified birds, while others did "bug mapping" among the grass roots. Our cheeks glowed, and that fresh-air smell that one enjoys on sheets that dried in the sun permeated our hair and clothing. I not only felt invigorated to be outside, I was also

Figure 5.3. Stream Fest Schedule

| 10:30–10:50 | Lunch and getting acquainted | | | | | |
| 10:50–11:00 | Introductions and getting started | | | | | |

	Orange	Pink	Lavender	Lime	Yellow	Blue
11:00–11:35	A1	B1	C1	A2	B2	C2
11:40–12:15	B1	C1	A1	B2	C2	A2
12:20–12:55	C1	A1	B1	C2	A2	B2

12:55–1:00	Closing

A1 = Stream (Mrs. Geddes, Mrs. Wong)
A2 = Stream (Mrs. Kress, Mrs. Holmes)
B1 = Environmental game (Mrs. Shrake)
B2 = Environmental game (Mr. Zimmerman)
C1 = Nature (Mr. Stevens)
C2 = Nature (Ms. D'Amelio)

awestruck by the bonds the children were forming and their renewed wonder at the world around them. How was it possible that strangers could work and learn together so well?

When the students had first met that day, they shyly eyed each other. Naturally wanting to stick with their friends, they cautiously approached the pals they had been getting to know through letters. Their timidity did not last very long, however, because the environmental activities we had planned broke the ice. One of my most uplifting memories is of one of my students, whose effervescent personality had not been appreciated by his classmates. He was the hit of his color group and was beaming by the time the group arrived at my station. Because his new friends so admired him, his classmates were able to see him in a new light.

The schedule in Figure 5.3 reflects the one we're happiest with after years of fine-tuning. In our first Stream Fests many of the stations were staffed by volunteers, including a bird expert from the Audubon Society, a scientist from DEP, and a parent who happens to be a fabulous science teacher. However, as we crammed more and more activities into the fest, children had less time at each station. Often, groups did not finish an activity within the allotted time frame, making them late for their next activity. Eventually, we decided to lengthen the time at each station and limit the number of activity periods to three.

Despite initial logistical problems, the four of us were excited about the overwhelming success of our fest. We each invited our grade-level teammates at our home schools to join in our venture the following year. We helped our colleagues set up key pal teams. They would get substitutes and join our Stream Fest, and we would do likewise for theirs. In this way we were able to double the number of students from our schools who were learning how to monitor streams.

Developing Stream Stewardship

Meanwhile, we continue to study our own streams. As students, parents, siblings, and teachers hunch over the nets together, fun and hard work blend into civic pride. The students begin to take ownership of the stream. I feel a deep sense of gratification when I hear the passion in their voices. ("Mrs. Shrake! Mr. Z! Just look at the trash over there! Can we clean it up?" We never visit the stream without trash bags.)

Connections and questions arise naturally. For example, we once discovered unusual amounts of dissolved nitrates and phosphates in the water and began to wonder how they got there. The children developed their own theories. Maybe the chemicals came from fertilizer on nearby lawns (possibly even their own) or detergents rinsed into storm drains after people washed their cars. This led students to discuss with their parents some of the ways they could cut back on their own contribution to the pollution. After all, this stream flows through their neighborhood and eventually into the Chesapeake Bay.

Back in school we learned how our tributary is connected to the Bay by tracing the path the water takes from the Paint Branch to Indian Creek to the Anacostia River, the Potomac River, and finally "the great shellfish bay," the Chesapeake. In the classroom, the Bay seems so distant, but being at the stream makes one feel much closer to it. No longer is "Save the Bay" an abstract catchphrase but a pledge to which the students devote themselves.

Perpetual Inquiry

Fellow ESIP teacher Jeanne Reardon imposes three criteria on the science activity she engages her students in: it must be, "real, relevant, and rigorous" (Saul and Reardon 1996, p. 18). Now, as our students engaged in authentic activity, my colleagues and I were driven to ask more questions. How is our monitoring of the stream helpful? Is it just an exercise to build the students' awareness and sense of civic duty? What do we do with the data that we are gathering? It might be interesting to compare fall and spring data, but so what—of what use would that be?

At the time we were "getting our feet wet," our county's DEP was reaching out to the school system. Ours were certainly not the first schools to establish stream teams, but the department was hoping to increase the number of school stream teams throughout the county and coordinate the data. Students were gathering and sending data to DEP for professional scientists to analyze. It was exciting to know that other elementary and secondary students were out there working together toward a common goal. The sponsor of Paint Branch High School's environmental club and I established a partnership between our schools. Her students fulfilled community service requirements by helping my students in our stream studies. By having high school mentors join us on several field trips, students at all levels developed a sense of teamwork and a spirit of collaboration—*and* they were helping scientists keep our world clean and safe.

We didn't leave all the data analysis to the professionals, though. We could and did make conjectures ourselves. With access to four years of data, we hoped to detect patterns that would suggest answers to a variety of questions about other county streams. How were these other streams similar to or different from ours?

A county instructional technology specialist developed a web page so we could enter our data and read data from other streams. DEP provided us with a map of "stream team" sites. My students and I regularly accessed the web site and pored over the map to learn which parts of the county had reported poor, fair, good, and excellent conditions. We were doing the work of real scientists.

The Mighty Chesapeake

Becoming stewards of our stream was exciting. It gave us a sense of "saving the Bay." But just as the ecocolumns did not in and of themselves build an awareness of entire ecosystems, our stream team experiences were not quite enough. The children felt a connection to the Chesapeake Bay as they studied one of its many tributaries. In addition, most of my students have crossed the Bay on their way to the beach. The brackish scent of its water must have filled their nostrils as they inched their way across the congested bridge in eager anticipation of their destination. But they did not know the Chesapeake intimately. How could I make it real to them? I had to get the kids to the Bay.

The Living Classrooms Foundation (LCF) provided us with the perfect opportunity. LCF owns four vessels that are traveling classrooms, each with an extremely enthusiastic crew ready to share their expertise. I planned for a field trip as a culminating activity for our ecosystems unit; and, thanks to the financial assistance of a generous Chesapeake Bay Trust grant, we were able to go out on one of the boats. LCF's pretrip activities, combined with our own classroom lessons and stream monitoring, prepared us to make the most of this experience.

On the day of the trip, the crew welcomed us aboard and, after the explanations of appropriate behavior and safety expectations, we boarded the *Mildred Belle,* a boat operated by LCF, and headed down the Patapsco River. The class split into four groups, which then rotated to different learning stations.

The group at the stern tested water quality, performing the same chemical tests on harbor water that they had in the stream. The children were amazed to find that one spot near a factory was so low in dissolved oxygen that hardly any living creatures could survive there. This experience helped give meaning to both a previous classroom investigation (when they learned that boiling water depleted dissolved oxygen) and a social studies unit (when they studied the industries of metropolitan areas). Factories that use water to cool their machines are required to recool the used water before returning it to the Bay, but apparently, we surmised, the water in the area we tested was not cooled sufficiently.

By the time the third group had a crack at the chemical testing, the *Mildred Belle* had traveled far enough from the factory that the water conditions were quite different. It took only a second after Ned glanced at the dark-blue liquid in the ampoule for him to exclaim appreciatively, "Wow! That's really good!" He was so experienced with dissolved-oxygen tests that he recognized a good reading immediately. It did my heart good to see that our work was real and relevant, and had become second nature to the kids.

New Horizons

I firmly believe that when you are supported in your endeavors, as my colleagues and I have been by so many people and agencies, you are obligated to give back. In our case, we gave back by sharing our expertise and experiences with interested colleagues.

The fourth graders in all four schools benefited from their experiences on the Bay. Our mission to educate the youngsters was realized. However, my stream buddies and I felt we could reach more children by helping other teachers learn to monitor streams with their classes. We have accordingly joined forces with our county's DEP to provide several stream-monitoring training sessions.

In addition, although the four of us would like to slow down, one interest leads to another, and our commitment to our streams has led us in new directions:

- Patrick has taken aerial photos of our sites from the helicopter he flies.
- Sandi, Joanne, and Patrick have committed their classes to a shad project and to a horseshoe crab project.
- Sandi's fifth-grade stream team club has developed an environmental web site (http://www.mcps.k12.md.us/schools/westbrookes/).
- Patrick, Joanne, Sandi, and I will participate in a bay grass restoration project sponsored by Maryland's Department of Natural Resources and the Chesapeake Bay Foundation.
- I am participating in the Living Classrooms Foundation's Nitrate Net project through which we monitor the Chesapeake's "airshed" (the quality of air over the Bay) by testing rainwater for chemicals.
- A new colleague, Albert DuPont from Pine Crest Elementary, has recently joined our group and was instrumental in helping our five classrooms telecommunicate with one another. Our students were thrilled to be able to see their key pals without having to wait for a Stream Fest. They excitedly shared their latest science projects and investigations.
- Albert and I have just been awarded a grant from the America On Line Foundation so that we can set up video conferences from our stream sites. When one class is at the stream, students at the other school will be able to see the stream from their classroom seats. We can also connect with experts like Diane Davis at DEP for guidance and information while we are at the stream.
- Because our students walk the streams and learn about water quality testing from their Stream Fest field trips, fellow Burtonsville Elementary fourth-grade teacher Mike Zimmerman and I now take a volunteer group of students from all the fourth grades at the school, along with their siblings and parents, to the stream on a Saturday morning.

Bringing It Back into Focus

This chapter tells two stories of collaboration: one among professional educators and scientists, and the other among students learning stream stewardship. Just as students' inquiries drive their scientific investigations, teachers' questions lead to action research and professional growth. These two stories are so closely interwoven that the thread of one belongs to the fabric of the other.

The stream (or, more specifically, the study of the stream) was not the important part of the story of my growth as a teacher; it was merely the vehicle. In a profession where one must reach out for adult companionship, the support of colleagues is invaluable, and thanks to that support, I have grown in ways I could not have imagined as a pre-service teacher. My friends have helped me grow professionally and have touched me personally. I will forever be indebted to them.

In a sense, however, the stream *is* the most important part of this story. Our time on earth should be spent adding value to the world and its creatures. If we can induce in our children a sense of connectedness to the earth, we can almost ensure its survival.

The stream continually connects my students to the earth and to each other. Immersing our hands in its refreshing water, hearing its trickling and bubbling, losing ourselves in the rush of the riffles and the calm of the pools—all these activities draw us to the stream. The animals who live in and around it, the plants that grow on its banks, the pebbles and cobbles scattered along the streambed fill us with their beauty. How can a child who has committed him- or herself to taking care of a part of the earth grow up without compassion and a sense of civic duty? Today's students are tomorrow's voters. They will elect or become the policymakers who bring about change. By making their school experiences real and relevant, we shape the future.

Acknowledgments

The ideas presented in this chapter did not originate entirely with me; in many ways I am merely the storyteller. I would like to thank the following for their support and collegiality.

Stream Fest teachers: Ellie Collister, Lynda D'Amelio, Amy Di Giovanni, Amanda Freely, Suzi Keegan, Sally Sanino, Nancy Wong, and Mike Zimmerman.

Secondary teachers who have collaborated with us: Sherry Barr, Randy Blair, and Nancy Carey, technology instructional specialist.

Science coordinators in Montgomery County Public Schools: Gerry Consuegra and Bill McDonald.

Scientists at Montgomery County DEP: Sandi Burk and Diane Davis.

Resources

The following web sites are good sources of further information on the ideas presented in this chapter:

Burtonsville Elementary School:
<http://www3.mcps.k12.md.us/schools/burtonsvillees/>
Chesapeake Bay Trust: <http://www2.ari.net/cbt/wwwhome.html>
Living Classrooms Foundation: <http://livingclassrooms.org/map.html>
Maryland Department of Natural Resources:
<http://www.dnr.state.md.us/>
Montgomery County DEP: <http://www.co.mo.md.us/dep/>
Save Our Streams/The Izaak Walton League of America:
<http://www.people.Virginia.EDU/~sos-iwla/Stream
Study/StreamStudyHomePage/StreamStudy.HTML>
Westbrook Elementary School:
<http://www.mcps.k12.md.us/schools/westbrookes/>

CHAPTER 6

Seeing Science in a New Light

SHARON ROBINSON-BOONSTRA

I HAVE TAUGHT middle school science for eighteen years, and over that period of time I've worked hard to ensure that my teaching practice continues to evolve and improve. I've attended conferences and workshops; I've read books; I've explored the strategies promoted by numerous educators and researchers. Through it all, I've discovered that the programs that most favorably affect my planning, teaching, and assessment of science are those that challenge my thinking and encourage me to reflect on my personal interpretation of science and education.

The Challenge

In 1994, I joined the Elementary Science Integration Project (ESIP) in order to work with other educators interested in science and curricular integration. I'd already been exploring my own ideas about inquiry and knew that I wanted my students more involved in authentic exploration. Although I'd incorporated inquiry-based investigations into many of my seventh- and eighth-grade science units, I was not entirely satisfied. I didn't want just "hands-on minds-on"—I wanted my students involved in *true* science.

I had had some success. For example, I developed an earthquake unit that incorporated multidisciplinary learning stations. I was pleased with the unit, and the students found the experience so meaningful they were still talking about it four years later. I conducted an annual outdoor-education program for the eighth graders. Each year, we camped out on an island, explored its environment, and met a series of outdoor challenges. The students were highly invested and involved in their investigations and found the experience both meaningful and memorable.

This was a start, but I wanted more. In fact, I felt guilty that I was unable to set up legitimate scientific experiments in my earth and environmental science units of study. I wanted to promote investigations that were truly experimental in nature—ones in which students developed procedures based on their own questions; controlled the variables, learning to change one variable at a time; collected data that was real; and formed conclusions based on their collected data.

This was the scientific model of science with which I had been raised. Like most other high school students of my day, I was taught (and praised when I used) the "scientific method." When I went on to study zoology in college, I was expected to conduct my increasingly sophisticated controlled experiments in the same manner. My final college lab research was on sea urchins. I removed them from their natural surroundings; and then, carefully controlling variables, I developed and implemented a study of their feeding preferences. I was a successful student—and a successful scientist—because I was in complete control of the experiment.

Control. We've been taught that this is the key to "good" science and the mark of a good scientist. Even the youngest children perceive scientists as adults (probably white males) wearing lab coats, measuring and mixing substances in laboratories. The image here is clear: the scientist is in control of the experiment.

I had no problem with this model as I taught the life sciences. In fact, I developed a number of engaging investigations through which students could develop and conduct their own tests and control variables. For example, in one popular lab, my students identified and experimented with factors that affect pulse rates. They carefully controlled the variables and then drew conclusions based on their collected data. In another set of investigations, students experimented with protozoan in grass and water mixtures while learning how to change single variables such as the amount of light or type of water. In both lessons, the student-scientists were encouraged to identify their own testable questions, develop an investigative plan, and conduct their own test, all within the context of the lesson. These life science activities provided the children with varied opportunities to experience scientific inquiry while promoting their roles as scientists in control of their investigations.

But I wondered: Is there a way I could incorporate these same principles into earth and environmental science, or was I simply trying to fit a square peg into a round hole?

New Light

During my first ESIP summer, noted astronomer Vera Rubin visited the program and spoke about her work and methodology. Little did she know that her talk about distant galaxies and mysterious dark matter would flip the switch and light the bulb over my head! "Astronomy," she told us, "is an observational, not an experimental, science."

That was it!

Many branches of science, like those in which I was engaging my eighth-grade earth and environmental science students, were primarily observational in nature. *I'd been trying to have my students explore an observational science through an experimental model.* It was not possible.

Scientists cannot change a variable during an earthquake to see what happens. They must wait for the earth to quake and then make careful observations. They cannot remove all the blue crabs from the Chesapeake Bay to see how the system would change if the crabs were extinct. They must observe the system intact.

We are not, nor can we be, in control of the natural world. We need to observe what is already here. Dr. Rubin's casual comment provided the key to solving my dilemma. I finally realized that in experimental sciences, the scientist is the manipulator, while in observational sciences, nature is the manipulator.

What a relief! I could now go back and address my earth and environmental science teaching completely differently. I no longer needed to feel guilty.

The observational sciences, of course, are not new and are actually known by a variety of names. Stephen Jay Gould and his Harvard colleagues refer to them as the "historical sciences." Others call them "naturalistic science." But for me, the term "historical" creates images of thick, dusty books, and "naturalistic" brings to mind visions of Victorian women who, lacking anything better to do, sit amid the flowers and sketch butterflies. So, even though those books provide important information, and a few of those Victorian women made significant scientific contributions, I find the adjective "observational" to be more meaningful.

As its name implies, this science emphasizes the importance of making careful and detailed observations, but it is critical to note that observational science is more than simply the act of observing. That is not science. Science needs to go somewhere. I believe that science is not a noun, it is a verb. It is action. So I want to make certain that students do not see observation as an end unto itself.

Observations, no matter how simple or complex, form the beginning of an exciting learning cycle. Students develop questions and hypotheses based upon their observations. These ideas, in turn, serve as a basis for more observations. This second round of observations might range from something as simple as taking a "closer look" to something as involved as collecting complex data. Learners begin to see patterns and/or relationships within the information collected. Does the accrued data support their original hypothesis? Should they modify their search? Should they begin again? What conclusions can they formulate? What new questions do they have?

As students generate new questions, they are spurred into new cycles of observation. This is what science is all about, what pushes science and scientists forward—the ongoing cycle of observing, questioning, hypothesizing, observing again, analyzing, observing again, forming conclusions, asking more questions, and observing again. Over and over and over.

Observational science can, and should, be incorporated into science classes at any grade level, varying in complexity with the needs, interests, and skills of the student-scientists. For example, after carefully observing the plants that surround their school, six-year-olds will notice similarities and differences, begin to draw conclusions, and be driven to ask new questions. Which plants grew in the sun and which in the shade? Were there any plants found in both sunny and shady areas? When was it sunny—in the morning or the afternoon? How moist was the ground in the shady area? How did that compare with the sunny location? Where were the tallest plants found? Suddenly, the students have a reason to return to the site and make a new round of more extensive observations. Older students may observe the same site, but their questions, and therefore their observations, will be more complex. For example, an advanced biology class might decide to calculate both the plant diversity and insect diversity in the area and then look for correlations by statistically analyzing the data.

Incorporating New Ideas

Since I first recognized the role of observation, I've been incorporating it throughout my curriculum. This model of scientific inquiry is particularly evident when I take my students on extended camping trips to study the estuary ecosystem of the Chesapeake Bay. Seventh graders camp at Point Lookout State Park on the Potomac River for four days. Eighth-grade students spend six days on an island on the Eastern Shore of Maryland. The focus of both trips is environmental observation, particularly as applied to plant and animal life.

The Seventh-Grade Trip

Before leaving for Point Lookout State Park, each seventh-grade student is assigned one Chesapeake Bay organism for which he or she will become the expert and prepare a report to share with the rest of the class during the trip. This report contains information on how to identify the organism, where it is likely to be found within the Bay's ecosystem, how it obtains energy, and at least one other special fact. (The instructions I give the seventh graders are shown in Figure 6.1.) The report serves several purposes.

1. It initiates literature-based research before we even leave for the trip.
2. Because no one can be an expert on every organism, it shares the wealth of knowledge and responsibility of research.
3. It develops students' expectations of what they will encounter on the trip.
4. It helps to focus student observations.

Once we are at our campsite, each student is assigned a time to present his or her report. Reports are usually given during breaks between other activities, before or after meals, or in the evening around the campfire. By the time we have completed the full round of reports, everyone is an expert on one organism, is knowledgeable about many, and begins to see the interrelationships among them all.

In the course of our stay at Point Lookout, the students and teachers are watching closely for the forms of life they have been learning about from the reports. It's amazing just how excited seventh-grade students can get when they actually find "their" organism. I'll always remember the girl who, after hearing the song of a Carolina wren, came running up to me yelling, "I heard it! I heard it! The cheeseburger bird." She called it the "cheeseburger bird" because to her it sounded like it was repeating "cheeseburger, cheeseburger, cheeseburger." Although I was surprised, I was far less concerned that she learned the real name of the bird than the fact that she was so excited about hearing it. Names are quickly forgotten, and easily retrieved from a field guide; the excitement of discovery lasts forever.

I think carefully before assigning animals. The ones we all know—red fox, great blue heron, bald eagle—are ecosystem celebrities, majestically taking their place at the top of the food chain. But it is the little organisms, such as barnacles, that I see as the unsung heroes of the ecosystem. Observing them encourages students to appreciate the complex workings of the entire system.

At one point during a seventh-grade trip, the children and I lie on our bellies and look over the side of a cement pier. We watch barnacles filter food from the water using their specialized filter-feeding apparatus. My students refer to this as "barnacling," the work of being a barnacle. I

Figure 6.1. Point Lookout: Instructions for Organism Identification and Report

---

In preparation for the trip to Point Lookout, you must prepare an identification poster and a short report on the organism that you have chosen. These will be presented to the group while we are at Point Lookout.

Poster   The poster must be a large colored drawing on a sheet of paper or poster board at least 18 by 24 inches. It is understood that you are not professional artists. The main goal of the poster will be to teach others what the organism looks like so that they can identify it if they see it during the trip. You need to describe the size of the organism. In addition, point out any special features, such as the white head of a mature bald eagle or the tiny silver line on the small fish called a silversides. Identify what makes your organism different from others similar to it.

Report   Be prepared to describe:
- Both the common name and the scientific name of the organism.
- Where we are likely to find your organism. For example, is it a bird that fishes in the water and therefore will likely be found around the water? Is your plant one that you are likely to find in the woods rather than by the water?
- What it eats or how it gets its energy.
- What its call or song sounds like.
- One other special fact about your organism.

You must research your poster and report. You may use the school library resources as well as books located in lab C and in the public library. Try to use books and field guides that relate specifically to the Chesapeake Bay. The web is probably not the easiest or best resource to use. You will not be given class time to do this work. You may do it for homework, in study hall, or during specials.

---

often lie back and listen to my students watch the "barnacling." Invariably, their conversations evolve as they observe and question:

"I can't see anything."

"What are we looking at?"

"I'm cold."

"How long do we have to say here?"

"Is that it?"

"Is it moving?"

"Look at the feather-like things."

"Is that what you were talking about, Ms. R-B?"

"Where are you seeing it?"

"Can you move over so I can see?"

"Oh, I have a bunch over here. Come see."

"Are they really eating?"

"They are so cool!"

The experience is far from over when the seventh graders get back home, shower, do their laundry, and return to school. They collaborate on a master list of all the organisms they observed on the trip and then develop food webs from their list in order to explore the interdependence of marsh life in greater depth. It's not long before the child who takes on the role of the tiny grass shrimp learns that he or she is going to be dinner for everyone else! Students soon realize that disturbing a single link in the web affects, directly or indirectly, everything else in the system.

One year, the students were disappointed that I wouldn't allow them to bring back some little silversides for our classroom aquarium. But their attitude changed as they developed their food web and began to respect the important role even a tiny silversides has on the ecosystem. Appreciation for the system requires respect for all of the individuals that make up that system, so returning one small fish became an important gesture. One silversides in our aquarium would mean one less for the green heron to consume and possibly one more mummichog consumed by the green heron.

The Eighth-Grade Adventure

Eighth graders also prepare reports on the organisms that we are likely to encounter, but their projects are more extensive than those written by students in the seventh grade. In addition to the basic information contained in the younger students' reports, eighth graders must include information on the organism's feeding strategies and reproductive behavior, and an analysis of the organism's structure and how that relates to its function and behavior. (See Figure 6.2 for the instructions for eighth graders.)

As part of our study of the habitat of Wye Island, we collect insects and spiders and look for a correlation between the plant diversity and the insect-spider diversity. At night we bury live-capture bottles in the ground to collect anything crawling past. Counting and classifying the collected species gives students the opportunity to closely observe those little critters that some find scary or offensive. Few people cherish the spider that crawls across their pillow, but those who observe spiders in their natural environment are fascinated by them.

One year, my students and I gained new respect for these tiny creatures as we watched a captured spider play dead. Since one of my cardinal

Figure 6.2. Wye Island: Instructions for Organism Identification and Report

In preparation for the trip to Wye Island, you must prepare a three- to five-minute oral report on the organism(s) that you have chosen. Your report must include the following:

- The organism's common name and scientific name (genus and species).
- A description of the organism for identification purposes, noting any special characteristics (called field marks).
- A description of the organism's habitat, noting where it is likely to be found on the island.
- A description of the feeding strategies of the organism. What does it eat and how? Is it a carnivore, herbivore, or omnivore?
- What is its place in the food web? Who eats it? Is it a producer, primary consumer, secondary consumer, tertiary consumer, scavenger, or decomposer?
- A description of the organism's reproductive behavior, including the care of its young.
- An analysis of the organism's structure and how it is related to its functioning and behavior.

Poster   The poster must be a large colored drawing on a sheet of paper or poster board at least 18 by 24 inches. It is understood that you are not professional artists. The main goal of the poster will be to teach others what the organism looks like so that they can identify it if they see it during the trip. You need to describe the size of the organism. In addition, point out any special features, such as the white head of a mature bald eagle or the tip of a fox's tail. Identify what makes your organism different from others similar to it.

You must research your poster and report. You may use the school library resources as well as books loaned by your science teacher and the public library. Try to use books and field guides that relate specifically to the Chesapeake Bay. The web is probably not the easiest or best resource to use. You will not be given class time to do this work. You may do it for homework, in study hall, or during specials.

Journals   Journals are to be used to record the following:

- Notes of your organism report research and the report itself.
- Notes on other students' organism reports.
- Notes on the instructional sessions on Saturday and Sunday.
- Daily entries regarding events, feelings, observations, drawings, or anything else of interest.

rules is that we do not harm anything we study, I was very disappointed to think that one of the spiders had died. Finally, convinced that all of our jiggling and jostling would not bring the spider back to life, we put the capture bottle down. As soon as we stopped shaking it, the spider began to move. We tested this several times, jiggling the capture bottle and watching the spider "die" again and again. We became so engrossed in our observation of the spider that we kept at it for over an hour before we let the spider crawl away. As we walked back to the camp, one of the students said, "I never knew spiders were so smart." What I heard between those words was a growing appreciation and respect for a living organism that went well beyond the "cute critter" mentality.

The campsite slowly evolves as the days progress. About twenty-four hours into the trip, things begin to appear on the picnic tables—not your everyday things, but newly discovered treasures that have taken on new meaning for the students. Feathers. Bones. Leaves. Turtle and mussel shells. Twigs with growths. Animal tracks in plaster of paris and leaf imprints in locally dug clay. Even an occasional dead animal (which is quickly moved out of camp as soon as it has served its purpose for observation).

I believe that the students bring these things to the table because they want to move pieces of this newfound environment into their own world, blending the familiar with the new. In a way, they are inviting their neighbors to dinner. The children become part of the marsh community as they muck around in the marshes, and it's inevitable that they would want to bring parts of the natural world back into their human community. Some of their collection will make it back to school, but for the most part what they take back with them is intangible: their newly acquired knowledge and emerging sense of place in the world.

The camping trip is scheduled during the eighth graders' final days at school. Because there are no more classes after they return, I like to conduct a culminating activity of all we have done and learned about the island. So, in an action that is as symbolic as it is altruistic, we give back to the environment. In coordination with the Department of Natural Resources, we replant marsh grasses along the eroded edges of the island. This allows students to protect the living things that have gained importance to them, from the lofty eagle and statuesque blue heron to the "cheeseburger"-singing wren and tricky spider.

A Time to Observe

Watching the students' growing stewardship convinces me that I have added one more piece into my evolving puzzle of meaningful science instruction. I am comfortable with my recently acquired definition of observational science and know that it is built on a historically firm foundation. Science was founded on the observations of nature and natural phenomena. Darwin was an observer, as was Audubon. Teachers need to be observers, and so do our students.

I am convinced that observation is at the root of powerful scientific inquiry, so I don't want to neglect its role as I develop my curriculum and make my classes more inquiry-based. I want to find a balance within my science program that reflects all modes of scientific research.

Like their professional counterparts, students need to be first and foremost observers, not manipulators, of science. But recognizing the power of observation is not enough. I fear that we tend to push children too quickly through their cycles of discovery. There is no fast track that moves students through and past firsthand experiences. Children become aware of the rhythms of the natural world through patient, extended observation. The gradual changes in the sun's position; the cyclical shifts of season; and the disappearance and reappearance of birds and animals, leaves, and flowers can only be seen through extended and extensive observation.

Children who are intimate observers of the natural world gain a sense of appreciation and awe, that "sense of wonder" written about so eloquently by Rachel Carson, which sparks learning and builds respect for the environment. My students might not remember the names of the "cheeseburger bird" or the grasses that they planted around Wye Island, but I hope they will listen more intently to the birds outside their window, they will question more quickly the destruction of precious wetlands, they will pause more often to watch the geese migrate, and they will model these behaviors for their own children in the years to come.

Camping Trip Logistics

Taking students on an extensive outdoor trip requires a team of dedicated teachers and volunteers. At our school, two teachers coordinate each trip: one facilitates the science education while the other structures the camping and community aspects of the trip. Usually, there are five adult chaperones and about fifty-four students. All five adults help with the general camping experience and monitor students; but while four of them are also responsible for the educational program, the fifth manages meals.

Pre-Trip Planning

One teacher helps the students organize all aspects of the camping trip. In order to foster ownership of the experience, we make sure that all students take some responsibility. As a group they discuss and decide on personal equipment needs, community equipment needs, food requirements, food preparation and cleanup, rules, tent arrangements, science needs, and group entertainment. They then form and join committees. Meal preparation and cleanup chores are rotated through the groups.

On-Site Logistics

We rotate small groups of students (ten to fifteen) through the educational activities. For example, during the four-day seventh-grade trip, we spend the second and third days rotating the student groups through four two-hour activity periods that focus on the park's environment. Because there is so much to explore, we tailor the programs to the strengths of the leaders. For example, one adult in our group is a specialist in edible plants. Another specializes in canoeing and water birds. I focus on the marshes and the bird life. Finally, because the area is rich in Civil War history, a fourth leader teaches about the island's history.

All leaders promote student observation skills. We encourage the children to question, hypothesize, and seek their own answers. When appropriate, we share specific details and facts about plants, birds, insects, and animals, but we do not expect the students to memorize these facts for a quiz. It is far more important that they observe, for example, that some types of grasses grow closer to the water's edge than others or that some of the non-native grasses are invading the Chesapeake Bay's marshes.

The following is a typical schedule for our trips.

Day One
Depart between 8:30 and 9:00 A.M.
Travel time.
Lunchtime.
Introductory activity: Exploring the site.
Set up camp.
Snack.
Make dinner: Free time for those not involved in dinner preparation.
Dinner.
Clean up after dinner; free time for those not involved in dinner cleanup.
Evening will be a combination of reports on organisms and group games (soccer, flashlight tag, capture the flag, etc.).
Free time/snack.
Students in own tents by 10:30 P.M.
Lights out and silence by 11:00 P.M.

Day Two

7:00 A.M.	Breakfast crew begins making breakfast.
8:00 A.M.	Breakfast.
9:30 A.M.	Leave for first activities (group rotations posted that morning; all students rotate through all activities over the four-day period).
11:30 A.M.	Return from morning activities; lunch crew begins lunch preparation while those who were at the marsh take showers.
12:00 noon	Lunch.
1:00 P.M.	Organism reports/free time.
2:00 P.M.	Leave for afternoon activities.
4:00 P.M.	Return from activities and have snack. Free time/showers for marsh people.
5:00 P.M.	Dinner preparation begins.
6:00 P.M.	Dinner followed by cleanup.
7:00 P.M.	Organism reports and group games.
10:00 P.M.	Free time/snack.
10:30 P.M.	Report to tents.
11:00 P.M.	Lights out and silence.

Day Three

Day three looks very much like day two, except we usually go to the museum at Point Lookout between lunch and the afternoon activity (depending on the ranger's schedule).

Day Four

After breakfast on day four, the morning is spent breaking down the campsite and preparing to leave. We take time to share our memories of the trip before we head for home. We have lunch at a fast food restaurant along the way. Once back at school, the children clean the equipment and return it to storage.

Days Five and Six (Eighth-Grade Trip)

The eighth-grade trip follows the same general format as the four-day seventh-grade excursion. Our final two days focus on outdoor challenges, such as canoeing around the island.

Special Tips

Here are some helpful pointers to keep in mind when planning an outdoor stay.

Supplies Besides the usual camping gear, it is important to bring extras of almost everything, especially batteries and matches. Large plastic bags and duct tape are also essential. Extra school supplies come in handy: drawing paper, markers, clipboards, and notebooks. It's important to be prepared for those unexpected scientific investigations in which students will undoubtedly become engaged, so I make sure we bring a variety of measuring tools, extra self-sealing plastic bags for collecting samples, magnifying devices, and thermometers.

Rainy Days   Rainy days happen, and it's best to be prepared for them. They require energy, flexibility, and a sense of humor. We always bring a collection of extra foul-weather gear: raincoats, wool sweaters, old jackets, shirts, and pants. (We've accumulated these unclaimed lost and found items over the course of many years.) *Be sure to store these in a waterproof bag!*

Our activities are rarely restricted by rain, except during thunderstorms when we do not permit students out of the camp area. On a rainy day we assess which activities need to be cancelled or modified due to wet conditions or low temperatures, then we head out into the weather. We feel that it's important for students to deal with some discomfort and realize that they are indeed "waterproof."

It's amazing how enjoyable rainy days can be when you are prepared. I always bring a variety of activities that are suitable for doing under a tarp or in tents. Sometimes we use this time for student presentations or for designing "fantasy organisms" that will adapt to the estuary environment.

With a large enough tarp, we can get fairly active. For example, we might create a food web of all the organisms we have studied. We would tie a string between the student who reported on the great blue heron and the student who reported on the mummichog, then connect the "mummichog" to the "grass shrimp" and the "grass shrimp" to the "green heron." Yes, this makes for an incredible tangle of string—that's the point! Through this activity, the students get to see how everything is connected.

Safety   We do return early from our trips when weather has become a safety issue. Hypothermia can be a real problem, even when the temperature is relatively mild. Children *and adults* can become hypothermic even in 60-degree temperatures if they are wet and do not have the proper clothing.

We always carry enough gear so that each activity group has its own first-aid fanny pack. We have emergency cellular phones at the main camp and make sure to have enough vehicles to transport a child home or to the hospital without impinging on the other students' program.

It is important to bring enough chaperones for two adults to leave at any time—one to drive and one to sit with and monitor an injured child. One year a child was seriously injured. It was imperative that two adults take him to the hospital, but we also needed to keep the program going for the other fifty students. Chaperones left behind at camp quickly shifted assignments to fill in the holes left by those missing. The day went on.

Keys for a Successful Trip

In short, here are the main ingredients of a successful trip:

- Help students develop a sense of ownership of the trip.
- Make use of leaders' talents.
- Give students space and time to socialize and play so that they are better able to focus on their work during the science activities.
- Give chaperones private space and time as well.
- Do not make the meals for the students. Cooking a meal for over fifty people can be a wonderful learning experience for them.
- Don't rely on macaroni and cheese or peanut butter and jelly. Make good meals a part of the experience.
- Focus on observing and appreciating the environment throughout your stay.
- Share your own questions about nature, your own growing sense of wonder.
- The trip should be fun. Enjoy the kids! Enjoy yourself!

CHAPTER 7

Getting a Lot from a Lot

Michael Rest

I**T'S JUNE, THE END** of the school year. My fifth-grade students and
I are closing the door on two years together as we dedicate the renovated lot across from Harlem Park Elementary School. Looking over the
tiny nursery of trees, vegetables, and flowering plants, I doubt that I'm
the only one who is remembering how that lot looked just two years
ago—littered with old stoves and abandoned hot water heaters; trash,
glass, and knives; even discarded condoms and needles.

But my thoughts go far deeper than fading images of trash juxtaposed
against the thriving garden before me. I find myself thinking about my
journey through my first years of teaching and the children who led the
way. I'm struck not only by the strides they've made as naturalists, writers, and poets, but also by their growth as reflective individuals who are
able to think critically and act positively.

Discovering Harlem Park

My first visit to Harlem Park was behind the wheel of a delivery truck. It
was December of 1992 and although I had received a bachelor's degree in
conservation biology six months earlier, I had no idea of what I wanted to
do with the rest of my life. Driving through the streets of Baltimore gave
me plenty of time to think—time to contemplate my options.

One day, after delivering some blueprints to a site near Harlem Park
Elementary School, I returned to my truck and found several youngsters
leaning on its hood. I had some time before my next delivery was due, so
I hung around and talked with this small group of nine- and ten-year-old
boys. The conversation included pretty routine schoolyard gripes: they
didn't like their teachers, they weren't having fun in school, everything
was boring. But there were deeper complaints as well, ones that reflected
the lack of resources available in their neighborhood and a growing dis-
content with school.

I stayed around a little longer and before I knew it, I was discussing career options with the school's principal. Harlem Park, it turned out, was a Tesseract School, one of nine Baltimore City schools under private contract with Educational Alternatives, Inc. EAI offered a variety of staffing options and soon after I mentioned that I'd been considering a career in teaching, I was completing the paperwork for a position as an instructional intern. I was on my way to a memorable relationship with this neighborhood I was just beginning to know.

Harlem Park has a long, rich history. Older residents tell fascinating stories, many of which include local African-American firsts. It was once a hub of cultural activity in Baltimore's African-American community. Many black-owned hotels and jazz clubs surrounded the area, and stars like Billie Holiday were frequent visitors. But Harlem Park changed over the years. Many of its row homes are now boarded up, and most of the remaining houses have been turned into apartments.

Almost all of Harlem Park's students were African-American, most of whom lived with their mothers and extended families. Although some parents were working toward a GED, many were academically ill equipped to help their elementary-age children with their homework.

It was almost impossible to shield children from the neighborhood crime. Drug trafficking and shootings were not uncommon and often occurred within sight of the school. Too many Harlem Park students knew someone who had been killed or injured in some crime-related event.

Churches were critical to the fabric of community life. Almost every child belonged to one of the many established or newly emerging congregations in the neighborhood, and many attended church camps in the summer. Several churches were involved with the school; at least one congregation sent a representative to Harlem Park's School Improvement Team meetings.

After-school programs were offered by Baltimore City Recreation and Parks, the YMCA, and the local Girls and Boys Club. But few students, other than those whose parents worked, ever attended these programs. Even the youngest children just "hung out" after school hours.

Discovering Teaching

I began my Harlem Park internship shortly after the 1992–93 winter holidays. I expected to ease slowly into the job, but when my cooperating teacher called in sick on my second day of work, I filled in. It was trial by fire, a very humbling experience, and I couldn't help worrying about what lay ahead. As the year progressed I could see that teaching presented a fair number of challenges, but I remained convinced that Harlem Park Elementary was the place I wanted to be.

My second year as an intern was in a third-grade classroom, where I worked with an experienced and enthusiastic teacher. We chose science as the foundation for our classroom adventures and soon found that the more we stressed its role in our daily lives, the more the students saw it everywhere around them. They took the elevator and wondered how it stopped. They asked about the light switch or why the water swirled in the sink as it gurgled down the drain. They became a classroom of observers, a classroom of researchers and investigators.

It wasn't long before I was involved outside of school as well—coaching neighborhood sports teams, conducting family science programs, or simply hiking through the neighborhood and taking field trips around the city. The children were naturally interested in the world around them and loved to share that interest with others. I could see that learning doesn't just happen behind a desk, but takes place in and out of the classroom, during and beyond school hours. Although I had begun my teaching career inside the school, my real connections with the students began as I worked with them outside of school.

It was then, when we stepped outside the restraints of the classroom, that we really started to grow. We could be ourselves and share those strengths and interests that often go unrecognized in a classroom setting. To be honest, I wasn't yet fully comfortable in my role as a teacher, and these alternative settings freed me, permitted me to share my enthusiasm for science, sports, and the outdoors. It allowed the children to display additional interests and talents as well, and gave them the chance to introduce me to their families and neighborhood.

Beyond the Curriculum

By June of 1994, I'd completed my internship and the required course work for an alternative teaching certification. I was pronounced officially ready to lead a class of my own, and I spent the summer preparing for my third-grade assignment. I anxiously arrived several days before the start of the school year, loaded down with the books and materials I'd collected for the third-grade curriculum—only to discover that, due to unexpected shifts in school population, several teaching assignments had been changed. I would now be teaching fifth grade.

There I was, a new teacher who had never had worked in fifth grade. Where should I turn? What should I do?

Well, I did what any first-year teacher would do—I opened the curriculum guide that September and began at page one. This book, I'd been taught, would give me the prescriptions and formulas I needed to structure learning. It would tell me what, when, and how I should approach each fifth-grade experience. It would be my bible.

I closed the guide in October, knowing there had to be a better way. This just wasn't working for me, and it certainly wasn't working for the kids.

The guide didn't know my students, their strengths, or their needs. Only a third of these kids read at or above fifth-grade level; the rest ranged from first to fourth-grade reading levels. A few students were excellent writers, but most of the others had difficulty getting their thoughts on paper. Some of the less able readers and writers were articulate speakers; but others spoke rarely, and I found it difficult to assess what they were thinking and learning.

How would a one-size-fits-all-fifth-graders curriculum help my class of multiply talented and challenged students? I could rely on the guide for content expectations and resources, but I knew I would have to find something else if I was to make learning a meaningful activity for my students and teaching a viable option for me. I needed strategies that would allow for a variety of skills and abilities, and I needed approaches that suited my own teaching style. But if I wasn't going to rely on the curriculum guide, how could I make sure that my students met the demands of the mandated curriculum and that they acquired the skills they needed to move on to middle school?

Not knowing where else to turn, I decided to let my students lead the way—a pretty scary step for a new teacher. I was afraid to let go, to give up control; but, to be honest, I never really *had* control of this class. What did I have to lose?

I considered my experience of working informally with the children and families in the neighborhood and decided to start by building on the strengths of an already established student community. The children lived, worked, played, and prayed with one another, in and out of school. It was only natural that they would want to learn with one another as well.

Traditional school procedures require that children either work independently or gather in teacher-generated "cooperative" groupings to perform externally assigned tasks. This was not how my students worked to their fullest capacity. I could see that every assignment was already turning into group work, either small-group or whole-class activity. In fact, within two or three minutes of any task I assigned, the children gathered into self-selected groups. I believed that these interactions were generally positive, that they provided the children with opportunities to build on each other's ideas and questions. Rather than detracting from learning experiences, the long-established student-to-student bonds actually enriched learning.

I continued to base the content of our work on the mandated curriculum, but I became more reflective of my own strengths and responsive to the children's interests and needs. We lingered when we needed to linger, and we moved on when we were ready to move on. By June I realized that we had covered the entire mandated fifth-grade curriculum. Could I be as fortunate the next time around?

Focus on Inquiry

I was anxiously awaiting my second year of teaching fifth grade when, shortly before school began, *surprise!* My assignment was changed. I would be teaching fourth grade and, I was told, would have a unique group. The majority of the children had moved together as a class since kindergarten and had a reputation as an energetic and challenging group.

I had already heard stories about the group and their years together: who got along with whom, which students should be separated from the first day. Despite the fact that I'd made great strides the year before in valuing independence and creativity, I felt the need to establish control with this new group of students, so the children were greeted on their first day in my class with desks in neat rows and carefully developed seating assignments. I should have known that by the end of the day, the children would have redesigned the room.

In many ways, this class was far more ready to begin the year than other groups of students I'd encountered at the beginning of September. Since they'd been together for so long they already knew one another and had developed some sense of working relationships: they knew with whom they could work well and with whom they could not. It was up to me, then, to establish a plan, a framework, with which we'd progress.

I studied the city's fourth-grade curriculum and objectives, and noted that I could address most of the outcomes by focusing on the natural environment. It was interesting and real, and it would not cost much money.

Children Observing

We began the year by talking about signs of fall. I hoped that the children would talk about what they were noticing: changes in the trees, different types of weather. But their observations centered on man-made events and objects: broken windows, cars parked on the street. The children seemed cut off from the environment: they rarely noticed the trees, the clouds, the birds. Clearly, they needed to develop their observation skills.

This is where science begins. Students must be able to recognize what exists and happens in the world around them, first identifying what is normally in place, or growing, or occurring in their world, then making note of what is changing. Once patterns emerge, they become surprised with the unexpected. Questions arise. Investigations ensue.

I had to think of something that would help the students build these skills and decided to introduce observation journals to the class. Standing at a window that faced west onto Stricker Street, one student at a time looked out from the safety of the classroom and recorded what he or she noticed.

After five full minutes at the window, the first child wrote, "A man sitting on the steps." That's all—just "A man sitting on the steps."

I asked him for more and he replied, "That's all that's out there."

Well, okay. That was a start.

Now we would work on looking for details to add to their observation journals. If they noticed a tree, I'd ask them, "Tall? Short? Leaves? What color?" Soon the descriptions became longer, more interesting. They saw what was the same every time they looked out the window and they saw what was new and different.

By October, they noticed that the leaves on some trees were changing color while the pine trees remained green. It was hard to believe that they had never recognized this before, but suddenly they did and wanted to learn more. "What's up with those leaves changing color?" "How can we find out what the name of that tree is?"

I brought a variety of field guides to school, including an urban guide that listed birds, insects, even roaches. The students' observations became more and more detailed. The more details they noticed, the more questions they generated. Their questions drove them to the books and back to the windows. Suddenly, they started making connections. One child said while reading about trees in a field guide, "Wow, we have the same kind of tree here that they have in a forest in Europe."

First Steps to Community Awareness

We could practice observation skills from our window, but we needed to go outside to learn about nature. So, whenever our school schedule allowed, we took walking trips around the neighborhood. The only requirement I made of the children was that they record observations of everything they found interesting that day. While some students' observations focused on the shapes, colors, and composition of the buildings (we'd also been taking weekly trips to the Baltimore Museum of Art), others noticed the pieces of nature pushing into their urban environment.

Tavon became the classroom naturalist. Taking a walk with him was like going on an urban safari. He always looked past the neighborhood blight: the needles, the trash, the broken windows. He noticed the grass pushing up through the sidewalk, the leaves turning color on the trees, a pigeon feasting on sidewalk delights. He made lists of everything he saw, and if he didn't know the real name of something he found, he'd give it one. Newly discovered bugs became the Six-Legged Mosher Street Mosquito or the Calhoun Street Spider. He'd then rush back to the classroom, anxious to check our field guides for the real names and more information.

We stayed close to the school that fall, rarely going more than a couple of blocks away. Even so, our excursions were expanding the children's sense of place and neighborhood. Few of these children ever traveled outside of Baltimore. They rarely wandered—or wondered—much beyond Harlem Park. But these early walks helped ground them in the community, enabling them to see the school, their homes, and their churches within the context of nature.

A Fresh Approach

I enjoyed my work at Harlem Park, but by that winter I felt I needed a new outlet. So I began working with the Baltimore's Parks and People Foundation and soon became part of a group called the Tree Tribe, a grassroots project aimed at urban greening. This was a perfect match, one that allowed me to get back to my roots as a conservation biologist, learn a little about urban forestry, meet some adults with whom I held common interests, and still take something back to the Harlem Park community.

Members of the Tree Tribe were challenged to initiate an urban greening project, no matter how small—plant one tree on a sidewalk, clean up a school ground, work in a park. I started thinking. What could I do that would benefit the project, the school, the neighborhood, and—most importantly—the kids?

Several ideas sprang to mind, but I believed that, if I were going to involve the students in a long-term community-based project, the idea must originate, at least in part, from the neighborhood children themselves. It was not my place to drive into Harlem Park and say, "Hey, you guys should clean this up and you should plant a tree here and you should grow something there."

Even so, I did have an idea. Across the street from the school was an abandoned lot where a church had burned. The building had been razed, but several feet of foundation remained, poking out from the earth. The lot was a repository for old appliances and trash and was often strewn with drug paraphernalia. I was chomping at the bit to take it over and make it into something different, something green.

Could I, should I, push the kids to take on a cleanup project with the lot? If so, how could I inspire them to action?

The solution fell into my lap in the form of a grant project targeted at Baltimore City youth. The Baltimore Community Foundation was looking for proposals from children who wanted to address a community problem. I brought copies of the "Youth as Resources" grant into the class and challenged the students to come up with ideas. We batted various suggestions around for several days and listed a number of viable ideas. Several students proposed school-based projects such as an academic competition or book fair, but the class as a whole wanted to do something more substantive, more community oriented.

Finally, one sunny March afternoon when we were outdoors playing kick ball, three or four students ran up to me and said, "Hey, Mr. Rest, some of us have been talking and we were thinking—see that lot across the street on Calhoun Street?"

"Where? Point it out to me," I said, knowing full well exactly where they meant.

"We have to walk past there every day on the way back from school. Can we do something with that?"

Eureka! For one moment, life was complete.

Making Plans

We had to move quickly. The grant was due on April 1, and we needed to get together a plan of action and write the nine-page proposal. The students had to identify a problem and then draw up a plan, a budget, and an evaluative strategy. The deadline was tight, and I was tempted to rush through the process, but we really needed time to prepare.

The first step was to identify a problem. Was the lot a health hazard, a haven for criminal activity, or simply an eyesore? Then, once we provided some documentation of the problem, we'd need to come up with a solution. What did we want in place of the trash in the lot? Why?

I asked the children to make drawings and models of how the lot looked now. I was taken aback by the results (and wouldn't attempt to analyze what they revealed about the kids and their perceptions of the community). They drew hypodermic needles, though none were visible from the sidewalk; and, even though we'd never seen a firearm on the property, a number of students included guns. This project symbolized more to these students than just fixing up an abandoned lot.

Next, they recorded how they wanted the lot to look after the project was completed. They started with basketball courts. *Domed* basketball courts. And swimming pools—*large, in-ground* swimming pools. I was surprised by their assumptions of what we could do with $3,000! But with these ideas we at least had a place to start discussing what we really wanted, what the neighborhood needed, and what was feasible in that location with the funds we were applying for. So we revisited the original problem and reflected on our emerging understanding about neighborhood and nature.

What was it that we really wanted? Well, we wanted something that would erase the ugliness and unhealthiness of the lot as it was now. We decided to start with something small and aesthetically pleasing: a simple garden in a small piece of the city.

We were finally ready to write the grant.

In response to the line "Describe the community problem you want to solve," students wrote the following:

> . . . trash, rocks, stick, boodles [sic], broken boodles, and other things. People put drug needles, stach drugs. Use it for a bathroom dogs and people have no respect for it. People sleep and it stinks and makes the community look worse. They put guns in the lots and rats are in there.

> . . . trash, glass, dust, drugs, homeless people, rats, homeless people sleep there, rats, people dump furniture and you see dead animals and people use the bathroom there and that makes the lot smell very bad.

> These lots are to not throw things that people do not want. I think that people should not put things in the lot like drugs, trash and people sleep there . . .

In answer to the question "What is your project idea?" they wrote:

Our project is to make the lot a community garden for everyone to spend some time and cool out and watch the sun and everyone can have a good time.

Our project is to adopt, design, and create a community garden and learning lot on the vacant lot on Calhoun Street across from the Rec Center.

We submitted the grant, but rather than sit back and wait for the foundation's approval, we decided to begin our work immediately. We were going to do this project whether or not we were funded.

I didn't want the children in the lot until it was relatively free of hazardous trash, so several adults joined me in an initial cleanup. The mess that awaited us exceeded our wildest expectations: several hot-water heaters and other large appliances, traffic cones and barrels, tires, innumerable bags of trash, bricks, bottles, broken glass, needles, and condoms.

We finished our first round of cleanup just about the time the foundation announced its first round of cuts. We weren't surprised to hear that we were still in the running. We were surprised to learn that the next step in the process required the children to deliver a formal presentation to the funders.

We went downtown together, but only the children were allowed to talk to the committee. Nervous, but fully prepared, the children presented the history of the project, the revised models they'd made of their proposed lot renovations, and their budget. They had divided up the responsibilities in advance, so each child was an expert on one area of the project. Although their presentation went nothing like we'd prepared, the children exuded an air of confidence as they explained every detail and answered every question.

There was plenty to keep us busy while we awaited the foundation's final decision. The Division of Forestry donated—and delivered—railroad ties and twelve loads of dirt. A fencer from the neighborhood provided chain-link fence. We spread the dirt, sunk the ties, dug holes for the fence. And we made plans.

Every task provided real-life problems to resolve in the classroom. We needed fencing, so we wrote letters of persuasion. Fencing was offered; so we wrote thank-you letters. How much fencing did we need? We calculated the perimeter of the lot. What should we plant? We read gardening books and talked to experts. When is the best time to plant? Back to the books.

Time passed productively; then, finally, the wait was over.

Growing as Scientists

It was late May when we got word that just 13 of the 120 proposals would be funded. Only a few received their full request, and Students on the Move—the name my students had chosen for our group—was one of them. What a marvelous way to end the school year! We had a check for $3,000. We had a clean lot. We had a fence and dirt and railroad ties. And we had the goodwill of the community and the commitment of students, neighbors, community workers, and friends to work throughout the summer and beyond. Best of all, there were wonderful adventures to look forward to, since my fourth graders and I would travel to fifth grade together.

But who could wait for September? The lot was ready and we were building momentum; a number of us decided to work all summer. I averaged about 35 hours a week, accompanied by a core group of ten or so children from my class, several of their siblings, a few middle schoolers, and a number of adults from the neighborhood.

We established a grassy area in the lot as our outdoor classroom. We bought a few deciduous trees so that there would be some color changes in autumn. We laid out a garden and planted a number of late-season vegetables. We tilled and weeded and watched our first crops grow and bloom. Best of all, we were establishing a comfortable place for children and adults to gather and work, or stop by and chat.

By the time school opened in September, we had a harvest of cucumbers, tomatoes, peppers, and green beans. We couldn't eat them all, so the children sold their vegetables to neighbors and teachers. We continued to visit the lot after school and on weekends, some children weeding or harvesting, others just "chilling" with friends or doing their homework.

Our first classroom-based project that fall was to build a composting site for the weeds and cafeteria garbage. This was a multistep process. First we had to identify the best site within the lot: a shady location where litter and trash wouldn't blow in. Then we built up the sides of the compost area, using reinforced lattice covered with heavy, opaque plastic. We gathered unusable garden vegetables and an assortment of school garbage, and mixed in leaf mold.

It would have been a great compost site if we hadn't continually disturbed it to see what was happening. The process was so interesting that we dug it up over and over and over again, checking out the decomposition of the material and the evolution of insect and worm life.

Our formal visits to the lot during the school year occurred less frequently than I'd hoped. Multiple demands on school time and a spate of neighborhood shootings kept us inside more often than not. But we did make time to get out when we could, and many of the students continued to join me at the lot outside of school hours. It wasn't long before we saw the effects of our experience permeating the entire school day.

As the children discussed what they were doing and seeing in the lot, I couldn't help thinking back to the previous year with these same children, when a typical observation yielded such comments as "A man sitting on the steps." Now they were asking questions like "Did you notice that the trees in the front of the lot are dropping their leaves faster than the trees in the back of the lot?" I also saw them begin to make connections beyond their immediate neighborhood. "I saw a tree in Lafayette Square [up the street] like we have in the lot. I wonder if it's the same kind."

The children's growth and development as scientists continued over the year. The project branched out in many directions, each more exciting than the one before. The students became fascinated with storms, and books about weather became staples on the classroom library shelves. We took several field trips, including a weekend camping trip to the state park. We wrote additional grants and got involved in streamside rehab at a local greenway.

Real-World Inquiry

One of the most intriguing activities came in the form of our own authentic environmental mystery. The children had been interested in trees since their early observations out the classroom window, and around April they decided that they wanted to raise and sell Christmas trees. But the foresters we talked with convinced the children that those trees would not grow well in our soil. So instead we purchased 200 seedlings, about forty each of five tree varieties. We planned a tree-planting party for an upcoming Saturday and awaited the arrival of the trees.

The seedlings arrived in three-gallon pots, all of them looking very scrawny except for the pines. The children were concerned about the health of the deciduous trees, but we all were confident that the pines would survive because they looked so green and strong. To our surprise, however, we saw buds on the deciduous trees within two weeks. Soon they were all blooming and thriving, but every single pine tree died.

Disappointed and excited at the same time, the children now had a mystery to investigate. Theories abounded: maybe the pine trees had a disease; maybe they had experienced temperature shock (they had been in cold storage and arrived very, very cold to the touch); maybe they were as sensitive to soil changes as the Christmas trees we'd been advised not to plant.

Conversations about pH, about how acid or alkaline the soil might be, evolved into action. The children dug up some of the dirt around the healthy pines that grew near the school and compared it with the soil in which their young pines were planted. Although we were unable to conduct a chemical analysis, they noted several differences in the soil samples. The new soil was darker, with more intact organic material in it. The soil around the older, thriving trees was more granular. Perhaps it provided better drainage.

We were not able to decide on an explanation for the pine tree deaths, but neither were the foresters who visited. The professionals agreed with the students, though, that the culprit was most likely the soil. Children are often led to believe that adults, especially scientists, have all the answers. It was empowering for this group of children to see that like them, professionals do not have all the answers either.

Moving On

The end of the year approached, and with it graduation. We dedicated the lot about a week before the end of school on a hot June day, the perfect kind of day for a small party in a garden. Students and adults had a chance to share their thoughts about the project. Student Sierra Warren wrote a verse in honor of the group:

Students on the Move,
Works real smooth.
They works when it's hot,
And work when it's not.

The 4th grade students,
in Harlem Park,
Decided to work,
They were real real smart.

They saw drug needles,
They saw weed packs.
So they decided,
To get rid of that.

The lot looked terrible,
The lot looked a mess.
The students saw this
They were upsessed.

They cleaned out the lot,
It looks real clean
The lot looks dandy,
The lot look lean.

The children talked about moving on to middle school, and I shared my plans about teaching in Asia for a year.

As we headed off in our different directions, I saw the lot as emblematic of our two-year experience. The children had come up with three words to describe their project: pride, unity, and commitment. Indeed, the lot unified us as a group; it provided a lab in which we worked together collegially for two years, and I think it will continue to connect us for many more, as the trees grow and we mature.

The lot provided a focal point for authentic learning for both the children and me. We learned about science. We read, we wrote, we calculated real numbers for real purposes. We learned about working together and working through problems. We learned to value community and gained a sense of stewardship for one small, neglected patch of earth.

I turned control of the lot over to the students, and as I headed off for Korea, I did not know whether I'd be involved in its future. But I did know that the memory of working there would always be a part of me.

Epilogue

I returned to Baltimore after my year in southeast Asia and accepted a sixth grade assignment at Harlem Park Middle School, a large building immediately adjacent to the elementary school where I began my teaching career. My new classroom windows look directly out over the lot.

Maintained by the community—primarily the family that lives next door and a number of the original Students on the Move—the lot is thriving. It is full and lush and filled with flowers, vegetables, and trees. Better yet, it has become a green place for people to gather: to garden, eat lunch, or, in the words of one of the original grant writers, "cool out and watch the sun and . . . have a good time."

I frequently see the students who wrote the grant, cleaned up the lot, and planted the original gardens and nursery. Several of them have been bugging me lately. "There's a big lot up the street, Mr. Rest. Wouldn't that make a great garden?"

CHAPTER 8

Taking Books Out-of-Doors

E. WENDY SAUL

T HERE ARE LOTS of ways to take books out-of-doors. The most obvious, of course, is to pick up a volume designed to be taken out-of-doors—for instance, a field guide. Undoubtedly such books are most easily read and understood while one is looking at a bird or a flower or a mushroom and trying to figure out "which one it is." Not only is such a book best understood outside of the classroom, but the outdoors is better perceived and classified as a result of the book. The connections are simple and direct.

Another way teachers sometimes bring books outdoors reflects their desire to celebrate a lovely day. When the weather is warm, but not too hot, and the ground is appropriately dry, and there is a spot in the schoolyard located beyond neighborhood noise and activity, teachers may bring a book outdoors and read it to the children. In this case there is little connection between the subject matter and the reading selection. The treat is being able to leave the confines of the classroom and enjoy the weather at the same time one listens to a good story.

Although I and the teachers I write about heartily approve of such activities, my purpose here is somewhat different. I believe that the reason we choose to read, to better understand and appreciate ourselves and others, should guide our reading about the out-of-doors. In this sense, taking books outside is not so much a physical act (that is, carrying the book with you when you leave the classroom) as a psychological act. Books that touch you and your students, books that become a part of you wherever you are or whenever you think about yourself as an inhabitant of the planet Earth, come with you when you go outside. They shape your experience of being out-of-doors. Moreover, in the act of reading and rereading such books, individuals can recreate and revive memories of the world outside, even when they are not able to leave the confines of home or school.

This is a tall order. How many books touch us so deeply that we are significantly changed by them? It is interesting to note how frequently and easily we assume that "multicultural" literature, for instance, will profoundly touch and change the lives of readers. Books about our physical world, however, are rarely considered "deep" or "meaningful" and are rarely thought of as "poignant." In seeking worthwhile fiction, for instance, we look for titles that invite students to recognize their own experiences or those of their families on the printed page. We also seek titles that invite children to share and appreciate the experiences of others in their neighborhood, community, region, or nation. Cannot those same standards be applied to books about the physical world? Could something called a science book touch us in a way that helps us to perceive the world differently, with new eyes and ears and hands?

Common wisdom suggests that the opposite is true. There is, for example, the traditional story about the centipede who is asked how she can walk with 100 feet. Why doesn't she trip? Which leg moves first? As she begins to think about her movement she finds that she is unable to move at all. The moral of this tale could be stated this way: analysis spoils everything of beauty.

William Butler Yeats was not quite so judgmental, but spoke in elegant tribute to what can't be explained. "How can we know the dancer from the dance?" he wrote. As a college student, I remember repeating this line over and over: "How can we know the dancer from the dance?" Since my primary goal as a student was to maintain an artistic sensibility, science appeared (and was presented) as a threat. I wanted the forest; I did not want to be lost in the trees. And as a young teacher I wanted to help my students to love metaphorical forests. Which brings us full circle: can a science book touch us? Can books about the physical world help initiate and promote the connection with nature that makes inquiry possible and ultimately transformative?

For me, such experience did not begin in a book. It began slowly, almost without my knowing it. Growing up where I did, when I did, everyone knew that pine trees were different than the trees that lost their leaves in winter. As a lover of words, I was pleased to find a name, a word, for the ones that weren't evergreens—they were called deciduous trees. And then there were flowers. Somehow flowers were so obviously beautiful that I never worried that learning their names would make them less lovely—the geranium, the chrysanthemum, impatiens, and phlox represented clearly different objects. To not know these names was like not knowing the difference between a dog and a cat. Some flowers even seemed to have familiar nicknames, like shooting star or sunflower.

Taking walks with a friend who loved to name everything, I noticed that trees, to him, embodied these same differences. I learned to differentiate between an oak and an elm not as an informational task but rather as a way of differentiating among neighbors. Later that information became refined; there exists a subtle but noticeable difference between a red oak and a white oak. Ferns seemed simple at first: the maidenhair fern was so easy to pick out; but later noting the specific attributes of so many different kinds of ferns seemed impossible. They still remain a blur. But I was no longer happy with that blur, with that nameless forest of ferns.

An educator and friend, Gary Heath, told me once that hunters are among the most ardent advocates of environmental education. At first I found this puzzling, but when I thought about it, it began to make sense. Good hunters notice changes in their surroundings; they know when the hawk population is down and the fox numbers are up. They also notice when the elms have died and what low forage begins to grow in their place. Their contact with the out-of-doors makes them conscious of change—of natural change and human-induced and -initiated change.

The other thing about hunters is that they are problem-solvers. To be a successful mushroom hunter, for instance, one must learn about cycles and spores—that morels tend to grow where elm trees have died, that mushrooms are most likely found in the autumn after a rainfall. As mushroom hunters look carefully at the ground, they see not only mushrooms, but also animal tracks and grasses and flowers. Wondering—asking questions—about how all these items connect is only natural.

You would think at this point that I have strayed far from books. Not so. What my frequent sojourns into the woods have taught me is that we remember and care about what touches us, what intrigues our friends, what makes sense and connects to what we know.

For many children, books can serve as a friend who makes sense, the one who is able to see what we often miss. Donna Dieckman, a teacher and friend of mine, grew up in the most inner of inner-city Baltimore. Everything around her was cement or paved-over blacktop, except for a single tree. In fifth grade Donna began reading Henry David Thoreau and fell in love not just with his language, but also with his vision of how humans relate to growing things. Sometimes with book in hand, but always with book in heart, she would study her neighborhood tree. It became hers, she told me, as much or more a part of her than the bedroom she shared with her sisters or the classroom she attended with thirty-some other children.

When Donna was a child, there were few trees in her neighborhood, and even fewer books for children that personalized the experience of looking at and living in nature. Fortunately, now there are many more such titles. These books can serve as models for those of us who teach, as voices for those who learn by listening and imitating. Here are but a few examples of books and authors who have touched my life and given me a different understanding of nature.

Seymour Simon has written over a hundred science books for young people. Some of them are about astronomy. Sitting here at my keyboard I can recite very few facts I have learned from Mr. Simon's astronomy books, so I can't claim that the facts themselves are what changed me. And if truth be told, I have always enjoyed going out on a clear night to look up at the sky sprinkled wildly with specks of light. Of course, in a physical sense, the sky I see today isn't radically different from the sky I saw twenty-five years ago, but after reading Seymour Simon's astronomy books, it seems different.

First of all, it is bigger. His books gave me a sense of the immensity of the solar system, and I can stretch my mind standing out there under the night sky, trying to conceive of how big the universe really is and knowing that I haven't captured even a drop of its immensity.

A second thing I've learned is that all those dots of light are not the same. Although Jupiter looks a lot like a star, it is not. When I look up I can now imagine that the hazy bands of light I see represent billions and billions of suns, some of which might have planets, but few, if any, of which support life as we know it.

I can also feel my feet planted on the earth and know that they are not really planted at all, but that they feel solid to me because of something called gravitational pull. And I know that there are people on the other side of our planet who are just waking up and who feel as solidly planted as I do, because of this same gravitational force, a force that exists on other planets in our solar system to a greater or lesser degree.

And I know that having these thoughts, and more like them, comes from having Seymour Simon's astronomy books with me out-of-doors, lodged in my own imagination.

A similar thing happens when I take a walk these days. I learn to cover my eyes with my hands. Jim Arnosky taught me to focus better using this technique in a book of his I read years ago—*Secrets of a Wildlife Watcher*. I see a bird's nest and a beaver's dam. And I look at them with the eyes of an architect, thanks to Jennifer Owings Dewey's *Animal Architecture*. I also owe her for my ability to think of the water in which beavers live as a series of habitats that support all sorts of living creatures. She, like David Macaulay, has taught me to think about the layers behind and below what I see on the surface (see Dewey's *At the Edge of the Pond* and Macaulay's *Underground*).

Books do more than provide ways to be and see in the out-of-doors. Various poems have given me metaphors that help me to recreate a feeling of being in the sun or wind or rain, whether I am inside or out. Langston Hughes has taught me that rain can "kiss you" (from "April Rain Song"); while Lillian Moore, in her poem "In the Fog," helps me see that fog "wraps you up" and then opens "to let you through."

Books can also prepare and guide us. Several years ago I visited the Everglades in Florida for the first time. I say "the first time," but that isn't really so. With Jean Craighead George I had traveled with Billie Wind in *The Talking Earth* as she explored the Everglades in her canoe. I had visited its backwaters through the illustrations of Wendell Minor, illustrator of George's book *Everglades,* and seen a rich tapestry of green that seemed so lush I almost doubted its existence. When I finally actually crossed a bridge and tramped through that swamp I was surprised by how still the alligators are and how noisy the bugs really are. But the surprises were possible because I had moved beyond a general impression of the forest, because I was able, through my experiences with books, to see both the forest and the trees.

We often notice that children in classrooms need to explore a set of materials and objects before they can begin any systematic investigation of them (Saul et al. 1993). We notice the same tendency while observing teachers like my fellow contributors to this book, but this time in terms of space. These teachers help children with both exploration and investigation, and are rewarded by children's clear engagement. Engagement with text is another way into science, another form of exploration. It does not substitute for the experience of being there, but books can help us begin, they may help us while we are there, and they surely help us as we go back to nature again and again with a heightened awareness of the world and of our place in it.

CHAPTER 9

Following the Cardinal

Deborah Galinski

Frogs and toads have short round bodies, large heads, and bulging eyes. Most frogs live both on land and water . . . Some observations we made at the pond were that frogs look slimy but they are really smooth. The first frogs you hear in the spring are called Spring Peepers. We have seen large groups of tadpoles and we have even seen the fish in the pond eat a few of them!

Frogs are in danger. Many scientists think that water pollution and poisons are killing the frogs. Another scientist we have researched, Joseph Kiesecker, has been studying what happens to frogs because of the sun's ultraviolet rays. He thinks that the rays pass through the eggs in the pond and change them. The rays change the eggs so that most of them do not hatch. Many of the eggs that do hatch produce deformed frogs.

—*From "The Hoppers" by Jaclyn Kreft and
Danielle Zaiser*

My story begins at the windows of my third-grade classroom and with a child's wandering gaze. I tried to pull Jason back into our group discussion by asking for his thoughts on the book we were reading. "But that cardinal on the window sill is staring at me!" he protested.

Sure enough, hovering above the ground was a beautiful, bright red cardinal that *did* appear to be looking in at the children! It was a captivating sight, and I, too, found myself wanting to drop my work to watch him.

The cardinal lingered at the window. I made a quick decision to have the children draw and/or write about the bird and, as always, record any questions that arose.

"Red bird watching, staring," wrote Stephanie.

"He looks like he is floating," added Nick. "Why doesn't he fly away?"

"Can he really see us through the dark window?"

Suddenly, our visitor flew off. We ran to the window and watched him head toward the woods at the edge of the school property.

"Can we follow him?" Andrea asked.

"Sure," I replied. We hustled down the halls and out the door. The children gathered in pairs and small groups at the edge of the woods, whispering and pointing fingers as they hunted for the cardinal. Although we didn't spot him (or any other cardinal) again that day, we spent about twenty minutes exploring the rest of the world outside our door. We returned to the room, and I asked the children to resume writing and drawing in their journals.

Philip had observed a caterpillar crawling slowly through the grass and wrote:

What kind of trees does it live in?
How does it defend itself?

Renee discovered a new bush:

What kind is it?
Does an animal eat it?
Will [the buds] turn into anything?

Many students were intrigued by the spiders they observed on nearby brush:

How do spiders make webs?
How do spiders make patterns in webs?
Will [the spider] survive the winter?

Becca recognized a robin, and wrote:

Why does it have a nest so low?
When does it fly south?
What color are the eggs inside the nest?

It was obvious that our brief outdoor trek had provoked both interest and questions, so when I heard a small voice ask, "Wouldn't it be great to go outside every day?" I was inclined to say yes. Instead, I answered, "Every day? No—but we *could* do this several times a month."

As soon as the words left my mouth, my mind raced with possibilities and potential pitfalls.

How would I keep the children focused while we were outdoors?
How could I help them develop their own questions about what
     was happening in their environment?
Would my students be able to design meaningful investigations?
How could I fit these excursions into my science curriculum and
     integrate them with Maryland reading and writing outcomes?

For what should I hold the students accountable while they were
  outdoors?
How could I assess my students' progress?

Taking Inquiry Outdoors

It was my eighth year of teaching and my second year at Manchester
Elementary School, a relatively rural school situated on the northern
edge of Maryland, just a few miles south of Pennsylvania farmland. I had
never given much thought to the importance of outdoor investigations
until that day with the cardinal, even though both schools where I'd
taught had inviting outdoor places to explore—places filled with trees,
fields, ponds, and gardens. My students and I had always conducted
investigations about the natural world; we had just never ventured outside to do them. For example, we explored animal habitats and behaviors through literature and through an *inside* investigation of owl pellets;
we explored the effects of salt water on grass growing *inside* a tank; we
investigated erosion through a child-created sand tank and rain bucket
inside the classroom. Now, as I thought about the questions that arose
from one brief excursion to the edge of the woods, I began to think about
the children's need for authentic experiences. I realized the importance of
exploring and investigating the world from *outside* the classroom.

As I began to plan how we'd conduct our outdoor investigations, I
was reminded of a colleague's comment. "Not only should children be
given the opportunity to observe their world closely," she said, "they
should be given their own place to do so." The idea of providing each of
the children with a location that they would watch over time, their own
"solo spot," was intriguing, I thought. This might be a way for individual students in my large class to personalize nature.

Rather than limiting their investigations to the grass or the log upon
which they sat, I would encourage them to explore anything they could see
from their spot. I hoped that, by doing so, my students would gain an intimate knowledge of one little piece of the world: how it responds quickly to
daily events like rain or sun or frost, and how it evolves slowly with the
seasons, gradually changing color and texture and the life it supports.

These are some of my observations from the first time that we went to
the outdoor classroom to adopt and observe our trees. The first day of
our adopt a tree observations was September 4, 1997. "We went outside
at 10:30 in the morning. The leaves of the tree I chose are very small. The
leaves of my tree are rough and veiny. The bark is thin and looks weak.
The bark is also bumpy." At first I thought this was a sassafras tree, but I

found out by looking at the flowers and leaves and identifying them in tree guides that it is a honeysuckle.

I also found out that my tree changes with the seasons. I noticed that the evergreen trees around my tree area did not change—they kept their green leaves and needles. In the autumn, the leaves of my tree turned brown and crinkled and began to fall to the ground. In the winter my tree had no leaves and appeared to be dead. I noticed that in the spring, my tree grew white flowers that smelled great! These are the honeysuckle flowers. Because my tree is still very small, it sways with the wind on breezy days.

—*From "Getting to the Roots of Trees"*
by Amanda Short

Planning for Outdoor Inquiry

Although I had high hopes for taking the children outdoors, I was experienced enough to know that this wouldn't be a successful or meaningful experience unless I found a way to establish purpose and order. We needed structure, or my eight-year-olds would turn outdoor free time into an outdoor free-for-all. I needed a starting point, and I needed some guideposts along the way. So, before deciding on the initial structure for taking the children outdoors, I took some time to think about my own practice and teaching philosophy. Since inquiry forms the foundation of my teaching, I am continually on the lookout for strategies that provoke and nurture children's questions. Solo spots, I thought, could be the newest twist to my inquiry-based teaching; but how could I build on my current routines to engage my students in this new adventure?

First, I thought about how I help children generate questions *inside* the classroom. Contrary to popular beliefs about young children, third graders are not always able to articulate productive questions. Sometimes the questioning process comes slowly to a child and some years, it seems, it is difficult for an entire class. Fortunately, my colleagues in the Elementary Science Integration Project (ESIP) and I have developed numerous techniques and strategies that I've adapted for my own use. The four that seemed to be most relevant for this project were question boards, inquiry sessions, journals, and scientists' meetings.

Question Boards Building on an idea developed by fifth-grade teacher Charlie Pearce (Pearce 1993), I maintain a "question board" on one wall of my classroom on which students record questions as they arise. (I allow the children to walk over quietly to the question board at any time, so that questions can be recorded before they're forgotten.) Questions emerge throughout the day. A high percentage of them are formulated as the children take part in science investigations. Many more arise while they are reading a piece of historical fiction, working with math manipulatives, or learning about their community in social studies.

Inquiry Sessions   I also try to work inquiry sessions into my regular weekly schedule. Ranging in length from one hour to all day, these sessions are self-directed periods of time in which students investigate one or more of the questions that have arisen during the week. Although the time is loosely structured, children know that they are being held accountable for conducting some type of research (through books or a scientific test), for collecting data, for recording their observations and questions, and for being able to share what they learned with the rest of the class. Sometimes I find it difficult to squeeze inquiry sessions into our busy schedule. I get more mileage out of these sessions if I look for ways to link science with other curricular areas. For example, I might connect student questions about structures (from beaver dams to skyscrapers) with a geometry unit by having the children investigate the strength and design of three-dimensional geometric structures as they analyze angles, count faces and edges, and compare shapes.

Journals   My students maintain journals in most subject areas. They often use double-entry journals, recording their observations on one side of the page and their questions on the other. Making note of mealworm metamorphosis, the flight patterns of different paper airplane designs, or the number of paper clips they can float on a square of aluminum foil without sinking often leads to productive questions. When children have difficulty completing the question side of their journal, I prod them with questions of my own. "What surprised you about that?" "What does that make you wonder?"

Scientists' Meetings   After an investigation in any subject area, the class meets to discuss general findings, specific discoveries, and questions. Not only do these meetings help document student work, they also are a breeding ground for questions and future investigations. As children share ideas with one another, they discuss, debate, challenge, compare, and generalize. I listen to their conversation and try to provoke new questions by asking things like "Did anyone get a different result?" "How could you do that differently next time?" or "What did you hear today that made you question your own or someone else's results?"

🍃

I wanted to build on these indoor strategies and adapt them to our new "solo spot" investigations. Our trips outdoors would be similar to our inquiry sessions, and I hoped that the students would draw from their inside practice of observing, recording, collecting data, drawing inferences, and questioning as they investigated the outdoors. Since the children were already accustomed to recording their observations and questions in journals, I designed a solo spot worksheet to help organize their thinking (see Figure 9.1). I kept the organizer simple so that observations and details could be recorded quickly and easily referenced later as children discussed their findings.

I decided to schedule scientists' meetings after each of our outdoor excursions. This would give these budding third-grade naturalists a regular period of time to share data, compare findings, and uncover the patterns of nature. I hoped the meetings would push the children to think about such questions as "Do I understand what I observed enough to describe it to my classmates?" "What details do I need to go back and check on?" "What research must I conduct to fill in the blanks in my writing, my drawing, my discussion, my understanding?"

With my loosely constructed academic plan in place, I turned my attention to a behavioral plan. As with indoor science, I knew we needed some ground rules before we left the classroom for our first solo spot visit. We discussed the need for quiet conversation and small, slow steps.

Figure 9.1. Solo Spot

You will choose a solo spot at the pond and at the outdoor classroom. A solo spot is a spot for you to enjoy by yourself. You will observe the life that is in your solo spot each month during the school year. It is your special spot; treat the life there with respect, and be careful not to harm any living thing. You are only to observe and record what you see.

September

Date:

The weather conditions were (write a few words telling about the weather conditions):

This is the spot I have chosen:

I chose this spot because:

Here are directions to my spot:

Map to my spot:

Eight-year-olds can get carried away with outdoor activity and I knew that the fresh air and open expanse of our large schoolyard were bound to invite loud voices and large movements, just the things that would drive away or, worse, trample the very life we were setting out to observe. We wanted to see as much as possible, and I knew that if the children raced to find a special spot, they'd miss the tiny details that compose the larger world.

Our list of rules was simple:

Walk to your solo spot.
Use your senses.
Record what you see, smell, hear.
Share at the scientists' meeting.
Be sure that you can see Ms. Galinski at all times.

Visiting Nature

Rabbits have two kinds of teeth. The teeth never stop growing. Other family pets get along with rabbits. A rabbit on the loose can find all sorts of things to play with. Rabbits can get to be 28 years old. Rabbits wait in a holding pen to be sent to laboratories all over the country.
—*From "Rabbits" by Danny Ditman*

After many discussions and some preparatory work with our solo spot record sheets, the children and I were ready to start our outdoor adventure. We gathered our papers, our pencils, and our jackets and headed outside. The children had little trouble identifying an "all-by-yourself spot" that interested them. Selections ranged from locations in the open field overlooking our large wooded area, to spots at the very edges of the trees, to spaces just inside the woods.

September 25
It's early October. The smell of "all" and the clear blue sky capture my attention. I sit in the open field under this beautiful sky—I can see over the hills and the tops of the trees.
—*From my own journal*

I knew I was setting an example that day. Just as I model the importance of reading and writing by reading and writing along with my students, I began to model the importance of recording my observations of the world around me. I looked around and noted that the children were as engrossed in their surroundings as I was. Everyone was writing and drawing.

Shades of red, orange on the edges of the leaves. Which color leaves will fall first? Crisp, fresh air—why do blue skies seem to smell this way? Chirping birds, flying from tree to tree—are they preparing for the journey south? When will they leave? Do all birds leave at the same time? A rabbit scampering through the tall field flowers—I wonder if any of my students saw that.

Yes! Danny saw the rabbit as it scampered in front of him. "Ah! Look! A rabbit!" he exclaimed. His squeals of delight frightened the rabbit deep into the woods, but for one brief moment, the entire class shared in the thrill of seeing wildlife up close in the school's backyard. Danny's first journal entries formed the foundation of his future research:

September 25
Does this rabbit live in the woods?
Is it male or female?
Does it have a family?
Was it really scared of me or just hunting for food?

We stayed outdoors for only ten minutes that first day, but we spent a full forty-five minutes sharing our observations and questions in a scientists' meeting when we returned to the classroom. The children's comments documented their enthusiasm for learning about nature and their capacity for careful observations and productive questions.

There was a tree with a huge hole on the side!
What do you think lives in that hole?
I found an insect nest! What kind of insect is it? Isn't it too early for cocoons?
How many legs does this ladybug have? Are they always red and black?
Will the leaves fall off this tree? They're still green.
Do spiders really suck blood? How?
Where does a grasshopper go when it's cold outside? Does it have enough to eat?

There seemed to be no end to the questions. We talked so long that we missed the first five minutes of lunch! Our conversation continued as we quickly cleaned up our materials and headed for the door.

Becoming Science Researchers

In our outdoor pond visits we write down what we find in a special journal. We write what the weather is like and the water temperature. We started our investigations when we found a fish and salamanders and some other animals. We observed that salamanders have a red stripe down their back. The fish in the pond right now are very small. We saw two water snakes and a lot of tadpoles too! We think that they are northern water snakes because they have black and brown rings around their bodies like the photographs we've seen of northern water snakes.

—From "Pond Life" by Dean Eby,
Allyson Thayil-Riley, and Dustin Shrodes

I was thrilled with the results of our first solo spot adventure and decided to continue these excursions throughout the year. Within weeks, I could see that going outdoors on a regular basis did more than provide a novel adventure for my students; it also fit in nicely with the academic outcomes for third graders in my district. The science-related outcomes were easy to establish: those outcomes that related to science content and concepts and those related to science-related habits of mind, attitudes, and applications.

The children were reading, writing, speaking, and listening for a variety of purposes. They articulated their observations and questions when we met in our scientists' meetings, and because the topic was of such high interest, they were attentive when their fellow naturalists shared their experiences. The children were also reading for information, and I could see by their related literature choices that they were often reading for literary experience. They wrote often, and I knew that the more writing practice they had, the better writers they would become.

When it came time for a more formal assessment, I surveyed the class to see how they would like to share their newfound information. We discussed several options—posters, charts, reports—but nothing really clicked. The children just weren't ready, and apparently they knew this better than I did. "I don't know enough about the life in my solo spot to report on it," Becca told me. What I heard in her comment was, "I need to know more. I *want* to know more."

So far, the children had been documenting their findings in a variety of ways, doing plenty of drawing, reading, writing, speaking, and listening. But it seemed that they wanted to take their learning one step further. They wanted to become experts in their topics of interest. They were ready to tackle more formal research. And I was ready to launch my attack. I scheduled a trip to the media center and arranged for our school's media specialist to demonstrate the use of encyclopedias and the nonfiction sections of the library. I enlisted parent volunteers to work with small groups and to help children locate information about the life they saw in their solo spot. I adapted my solo spot worksheet to reflect the children's use of resources (see Figure 9.2).

Figure 9.2. Life List Record Sheets

Name:

Part I
Today's weather:

Make a drawing of the living thing.

What is the name of your living thing? If you're not sure, then leave this blank until you research it.

Write three or more questions about your living thing that you want to answer.

Part II
Use a resource to learn more about your living thing. What did you learn?

Resource(s) used:

Throughout the next few weeks, we discussed the processes of writing as each child drafted, conferenced, edited, and published an informational article about their solo spot. I bound the articles into a book and placed the book with other student-produced works. The children began to read one another's articles and were making valuable links, not just between child and nature, but among the roles of scientific observation and documentation, writing, drawing, reading, and research.

> There are 50 different kinds of garden spiders. The web is 50 cm. X 50 cm. Garden spiders shake the web to scare you away. Spiders can produce silk all of their life while insects can only [do this] in one stage of life. The spinners are located in the abdomen. Almost all spiders have poison glands. All but 2 (black widow and brown recluse) are harmless to us. When spiders don't get enough water, their legs stiffen and they can't straighten them.
> —*From "Spiders" by Timothy Fischer*

The Next Step: Between the Cracks of the Sidewalk

Spring arrived. Ready for something new, we decided to take our Life List Record Sheets on one of our regular walking trips through the town. Although Manchester Elementary School is surrounded by open fields and woods, it actually is situated just off Main Street, in the center of a small town. Because of our central location and the safety of the sidewalks, I often guide my class on walking field trips through our historic town. Using the sidewalk as a starting point, I thought, might expand students' ideas about nature. We don't need to be in the woods to see birds and insects. Grass pushes through the cracks in the sidewalk. Ivy creeps through the mortar of old brick buildings. The bark of a single tree houses a world of insects. The tiniest piece of earth in the most urban of areas can be home to worms, ants, and spiders. The questions began where the sidewalk meets the grass.

How could trees grow in such a small square of grass surrounded by sidewalk?

We walked a little farther and discovered mushrooms growing in a patch of grass outside of the fire station.

Are they poisonous? How do they grow upside down?

Small insects were scrambling for cover between the sidewalk and the supporting walls of the town office building.

How do they live there? Where do they find their food?

The students were off on another adventure—new pieces of nature to explore; new needs for turning to books; new hypotheses to investigate, debate, and share. In the woods or on the sidewalk, I loved the authenticity of the outdoor experience and ended the year committed to making solo spots a regular part of my program. As the following September approached, I found myself looking for new ways to incorporate outdoor experiences into classroom plans.

Putting Some KIC into Outdoor Investigations

Once again, I turned to strategies I used inside the classroom to build ideas for outdoor practice. During our regular science periods, students were taught to categorize their science questions into those that were observational or researchable and those that were testable. "How would you find the answer to that?" I'd ask as we read the children's questions aloud. We'd then differentiate between questions that could be answered through research and questions that could best be resolved by designing and conducting an experiment or controlled test. I found that analyzing questions gave young scientists a starting place when it was time for an inquiry session: they could turn to books, ask an expert, set up a long-term observational study, or develop a test in which they controlled variables and collected data.

It wasn't long before the students took the idea of "testable questions" outdoors. Some students tracked the temperature of the pond and of rain puddles after storms. Others used hand lenses and microscopes for a closer look at insects, rocks, and tracks. Still others questioned why grass wasn't growing in certain areas of the schoolyard and looked for ways to remedy the problem.

> We found a lot of quartz and some iron pyrite. We also found some layered gabbro. We tried to find limestone by putting vinegar on different white rocks. We didn't find any limestone but we found some marble and chalk. We did an experiment. The ingredients were boiling water, granulated sugar, food coloring, and salt. We tried to grow crystals using those ingredients. At the time of [this report], crystals had not yet formed.
>
> We also tried to make a rock cleaner and a chalk dissolver. The ingredients were food coloring, salt, sugar, rubbing alcohol, soap, and cornstarch. We started putting the ingredients together to see what would happen. Then we tried to clean a rock, but it did not work. Then we tried to dissolve the natural chalk—it worked a little.
>
> Scientists next year can find rocks on their school property and observe them. We recommend trying experiments like the hardness test and the luster test.
>
> *—From "The Rockin' Rockies" by Adam Geiman, Joey Ottomano, Nik Shizas, and Drew Wagner*

I soon realized that our outdoor investigations would fit in nicely with one of my favorite activities: the Kids' Inquiry Conference (KIC). Each year, students from schools in various districts come together to share their science research with one another. Unlike traditional science fairs, KIC is modeled after professional science conferences. The day consists of breakout sessions, poster sessions, a keynote speaker, and perhaps tours of the hosting facility (often a college or science lab facility). Students present in front of their peers; are encouraged to bring overheads, slides, and videos to document their research; and share their data through graphs, charts, photographs, and demonstrations. Presentations are augmented by student-written articles, which are compiled in *The Kids' Inquiry Conference Journal.*

Our outdoor classroom provided a rich location to start new investigations for KIC presentations. Observations provoked questions; and questions sent the children to field guides, books, the Internet, and other resources. Developing *The Kids' Inquiry Conference Journal* articles moved the children through the entire scientific writing process, from field notes to rough drafts to final edits to publication.

At last our outdoor experience seemed full and complete. The children were making meaning from their encounters with nature and were learning to communicate their excitement and their discoveries with other student scientists.

Following the Cardinal

When I think back to a little red cardinal perched on our window ledge, to one child who was bewitched by its appearance, and to an experience that prompted me to move science, reading, and writing outside the classroom walls, I can no longer imagine staying indoors to study the outdoor world. But as a teacher, I must ask: Have we overcome the pitfalls that threatened to hold us back from our first adventure? Have we achieved the goals I established at the beginning? I considered a few of my original questions.

How Would I Keep the Children Focused While We Were Outdoors? Keeping children focused was easy. Just having them be outside and really observe nature closely was usually enough to keep students on task, but holding them accountable for their outdoor experience was critical. Each child knew he or she would have to share their discoveries and questions with the rest of the class orally during the scientists' meeting and in writing through journals and articles. The students quickly assumed ownership of their personal pieces of nature and were motivated to draw and write about their findings. I was pleased to see that they valued their own discoveries.

> Our school has a pond and ever since we started going there, we were interested in the little critters there. We go out to the fields, through the woods and threw [sic] a field. It is a lot of work. We have been visiting the pond for the past several months of school. We have observed the pond and it has been changing and changing when we have gone. We even have seen two water snakes this spring!
> —*From "The Pond Life Detectives" by*
> *Galen Blubaugh, Jonathan Connelly,*
> *Wesley Schwatka, and Danny Stone*

How Could I Help Them Develop Their Own Questions About What Was Happening in Their Environment? It was obvious from our very first excursion that the children were interested in what was going on outdoors. But, as with any period of inquiry, it was the repeated visits to our solo spots and the outdoor classroom that provoked the most meaningful questions. Building on the questioning practices established inside the classroom helped the children develop productive testable and researchable questions outside the building.

> The outdoor classroom is a place where we go to observe and record the changes in nature. When we began going outside to observe wildlife in the beginning of the school year, we also adopted trees so we could watch the changes of one specific tree. I adopted a honeysuckle tree. I chose this tree because it is small and full and very forked. I chose this tree because I like these traits of this tree. In result to my research and observations, I learned a lot of interesting facts about trees that I never knew before. I would suggest to future scientists that they adopt a tree in their school area. They should record what they see and do each month and be ready to see exciting changes!
>
> —From "Getting Down to the Roots of Trees" by Amanda Short

Would My Students Be Able to Design Meaningful Research and Investigations? The children's curiosity about plants and animals was well documented from the beginning of the outdoor project. Once again, building on my indoor science practices helped to keep students focused and behaving like scientists, and they were able to persevere throughout the question development, investigation, data collection, and writing phases of their research.

> Our topic is natural dye. Our questions were: What natural flowers or berries can we use to make dye? And what will stain? Our idea started at the outdoor classroom when we saw all the berries and flowers and wanted to do tie dye, but you can only do natural things so we changed it to natural dye. We used blackberries, raspberries, tomatoes, and mustard flowers.
>
> We used blackberries and raspberries. We used containers to hold the blackberries, raspberries, mustard flowers, tomatoes, mud, purple flowers, and beets. We put water in containers and smashed up the berries and other things. After that, we mixed up some different kinds of dyes. We tested out on a piece of towel that we had. After some mixing and swishing, we finally found one dye we liked so Georgia used it on her shirt and let it sit on a chair and dry. After it dried it looked really cool. We tried the blackberries, but it went through the shirt onto the front. Again it looked really cool. We went to the outdoor classroom and got mustard flowers, dandelions, and clover.
>
> These are some of the things that we found that would dye. We found that tomatoes sometimes it worked and sometimes it didn't. How we learned this is we got the tomato juice out and added water. Then after

that we tried the dye on scraps. Then we used it on our shirt. We also tried different flowers. They did not work. We also tried blackberries and red raspberries. They worked the best. We used the potato smasher to smash the berries. We did this in a container with water. Then we tried it on scraps. Then we thought that it would be a good idea to mix the two together. We also found out that if you make mud it would dye. Those are the things that will and won't dye.

Some things other scientists could test include using hot water, cold water, and vinegar. Next time we do this, we will use leaves, dandelions, other kinds of flowers and maybe different types of fruits.

—*From "To Dye For, Naturally" by*
Georgia Fringer, Lydia Hochheimer,
Caroline Martin, and Meghan Rippeon

How Could I Fit These Excursions into My Science Curriculum and Integrate It with Maryland Reading and Writing Outcomes?   The links to science were obvious. My students were spending time practicing the processes of science—questioning, collecting data, forming and revising hypotheses, drawing inferences and conclusions, and communicating their findings.

I could also see plenty of links with our language arts goals. The children were talking, listening, reading, and writing about the nature they were finding in their solo spots and at the outdoor classroom. This had become the perfect avenue for my students to read nonfiction and practice their expository writing skills.

We decided to catch and observe two salamanders for a few days. We set up a salamander habitat inside an aquarium in our classroom. The way that we set up our salamander cage is by first putting 3 cups of water in the cage. Then we put some grass and a piece of wood in the cage. By reading and observing our salamander we learned that salamanders' tails can break off. The resources that we used are books. We used the *Pond Life Pocket Guide* from National Geographic and the *Reptiles and Amphibians Pocket Guide* from National Geographic to support our research.

—*From "Pond Life People" by Dean Eby,*
Allyson Thayil-Riley, and Dustin Shrodes

For What Should I Hold the Students Accountable While They Were Outdoors? How Could I Assess My Students' Progress?   Students were held to the same standards outdoors that they were held to indoors. Not only were they required to adhere to specific codes of behavior, they also were expected to be actively engaged in observing, questioning, collecting data, recording findings, drawing inferences, and communicating their findings, both orally and in writing. Scientists' meetings, Life List Record Sheets, and research articles provided me with significant documentation of students' work and authentic work samples from which I could assess their progress in science concepts, vocabulary, and skills and language processes.

🍂

Teaching is an ongoing adventure. I was not surprised by all the children gained by taking science, reading, and writing outdoors. But I never anticipated the benefits to me as a teacher and as an individual—a renewed awareness of the natural world, and a heightened sense of wonder in the beauty and complexity of the schoolyard.

CHAPTER 10

Writing Out

KAREN PEARCE

SEPTEMBER. My twenty-five middle school language arts students sit outside at picnic tables, listening as the wind rustles through the leaves of the single, much-loved tree that graces our outdoor classroom. In their journals, the students are composing responses to the question "What is a tree good for?"

"Think back," I tell them, "and remember the unit you studied about trees and their importance in sixth grade."

"Why are we doing this?" Shawn asks. "This sounds more like science class than language arts."

Why are we doing this? The immediate answer is that the activity taps the students' prior knowledge and prepares them for reading the short story "Autumntime" (Lentini 1989). But the real reason for having science and nature in my classroom is much more complex. Working outside and focusing on ideas about the natural world may seem strange to the students at first. I teach science without invading other curricula or forcing issues. In our classroom, the lines between science and writing blur. Students come to value our trips outdoors as they value questioning and seeking answers. In our classroom, there are books, paper, pens, and dictionaries, but also fossils and chisels, batteries and magnets. At times, there will be leaves and bark, or limestone and beakers. In the midst of all this, I teach writing and reading, speaking, and thinking, and share my love of the natural world. And I teach science—because it is part of literature and part of life.

Why are we doing this? That is a question I ask myself often—about every activity and every lesson—because answering that question helps me refine my own thinking and focus on my goals. Infusing the middle school writing and literature lessons with science process skills and nature study is a result of many things—my experiences as a learner, an affinity for the natural world, and a commitment to curriculum integration. Teaching outdoors offers a chance to link all these ideas.

The Role of Novelty: Someplace Else

Traditionally, when we think of school, the image summoned up is a place: four walls, a ceiling and a floor, halls, desks, chalkboards. Learning takes place within these confines. But children who enter our schools have also been learning all the time in every place throughout their lives. Many of them learned something on the bus on their way to school.

Recognizing that students acquire knowledge in many ways and places is one reason that I use the outdoors in lessons. I learned this as a student when my own teachers did not stop at the doorway of the classroom.

In a secondary teaching methods class in college, my instructor often modeled ideas he wanted us to recall and use as teachers. Thus, his class was often a movable feast. We met in the assigned classroom, of course, but also in the library, in the dining room, in a lobby, and outdoors. His basis for this nomadic teaching style was that novel settings make people pay attention. We often complained about our wandering, but not seriously, because at heart we agreed with him. It was fun to take our classroom on the road. Often, our academic home away from home related to the concepts we discussed; just as often, however, we went outdoors simply because the world is a beautiful place.

These ideas—that learning takes place beyond as well as in a classroom, and that sometimes one goes outdoors to be part of the wider world—fuel my approach to working outdoors with students.

Early in the year, my lessons focus on description in writing and incorporate the skill of observation in science. These two objectives are so closely linked that the students do not differentiate between science and language arts. Over the years, my students' responses to these lessons have taught me a great deal. Our setting is the outdoor classroom at West Middle School: three picnic tables near a forty-year-old pin oak tree. The lessons help us to see the world with a writer's eye—to note color, texture, and spatial relationships—and to talk with one another about our observations.

The first step is to acclimate the students to working outside. This is required because sometimes novelty breeds chaos (or, as one teacher put it, "I'd like to do fun things with them, but they are always so difficult"). The constraints of our activity keep the chaos minimal, and my philosophy is that on-task talking is usually okay. The objective is to cultivate keen observation skills and to document our observations. We walk to the tables, sit down, and look around. Students are given three minutes for silent observation. They may walk around to select one item to sketch

---

Figure 10.1. Sketching Nature

Date:_____ Time: _____

Weather: _____

Use the space below to sketch an object, plant, or animal from the world of nature.

---

later. After three minutes, students may form pairs or small groups, but each must talk to someone to explain which natural object they will sketch. This discussion usually takes six minutes. Then they have time for silent sketching. (A form I use to encourage this activity is shown in Figure 10.1.) After twenty minutes, students share their sketches with one another and we return to class.

The next day, we begin with journal writing. Students address the question "What were you trying to do as you sketched?" Their answers are varied, ranging from "I was trying to show that the shadow of the leaf is just like the leaf" to "I was trying to show how many seeds there were in the sunflower." Without trying, these students have learned to focus their effort. The question underscores the ideas that drawing is composing and that purpose is part of composition.

Several days later, after reading a story rich in description of the natural world, we go outside again, this time with a bit more freedom. The objective now is to encourage the students to use rich, sensory words in their writing. They have six minutes to wander silently about, watching, listening, feeling the world. Then we talk about our observations. This time the students write instead of sketch, and the prompt is open-ended: "Use your senses to observe the world. Then write in your journal in any genre you choose." Some write poetry, some prose; a few write song lyrics to a tune they hear playing in their minds. Becky, for example, composed this poem:

> *Outside everything has a beautiful smell*
> *Under the tree a crunchy leaf fell*
> *The birds are leaving singing sweet tunes*
> *Silently caterpillars build cocoons*
> *I get a chill on my cheeks from the crisp morning air*

Days are getting short; the weather is fair
Each passing day brings a new sign of fall.
(I wish I could be here for them all.)

Becky used rhyme and alliteration in her acrostic poem. She implies a contrast between outside and inside. Her concluding wish is a poignant one.

Carly voiced the same ideas in a different way:

Outdoors I hear the cricket chirp
And the distant rumble of cars
Outdoors I smell the fresh cut grass
Compared to school, it's Mars.
Outdoors I see the blue of the sky
The green of the grass, the sun in my eye.
Outside I feel the wood of my chair,
The sun on my arm, the wind in my hair.
Outdoors I am free; I can run and play
I wish I could be outdoors every day.

I, too, wish I could be outdoors every day. My own feelings about nature are a compelling reason why our classes sometimes take place where the ceiling is sky.

The Nitty-Gritty

Departing from the traditional lesson plans and places of a language arts class brings lots of questions. Answering the question "Why?" is easy, but "How?" and "What?" take some careful consideration. Deciding *how* to structure ventures outside is crucial, because it involves issues of safety and management. Two guidelines help me to make our trips successful: *plan ahead* and *simplify*.

These two guidelines encompass many provisions. It is important for me to know at least a week ahead when I want to use the outdoor area so that I can sign up for the activity on the school calendar. I usually designate several dates to allow for a back-up day in case of bad weather. A day or two in advance I let the students know our plans and give them permission to bring a jacket to class if the day is cool. I always let the school secretary know when we leave the building and I post a note on the classroom door. These little steps keep things running smoothly.

Success outdoors also depends on keeping things simple. Before we go outdoors, the class generates a short list of rules; I add any that I see as important but that the students may not have thought of. Our rules usually require that we be quiet indoors while walking past other class-rooms, and they specify exactly where students may go once outside. They are free to walk and talk within those boundaries. Experience has also taught us to bring very little with us. Journals with a hard back are perfect for writing. For sketching, I provide unlined paper and clip-boards. Each student brings along a pencil or pen. All other materials are left in the classroom.

Here are some typical rules for excursions:

1. Bring only a journal and pencil or pen.
2. Walk quietly on the right side of the hall.
3. Cross the parking lot only on the teacher's signal.
4. Stay with the class while on the way.
5. Observe plants, animals, and insects without tearing or disturbing them.
6. Take examples back only with permission.
7. Acorns are for growing, not throwing.

Deciding *what* to do outdoors is also important. Most of my lessons arise from writing or literature objectives. Writing is often richer and more varied when done outdoors, so journal entries are sometimes our goal (Figure 10.2 is a journal prompt I used with my students). Another idea I have tried is to look for examples of literary concepts outdoors. We found the theme of conflict especially intriguing. In order to further their understanding of conflict, students looked for examples of conflict outdoors, assisted by the form in Figure 10.3. When we assembled at the picnic tables afterward, I asked them for a definition of conflict. "A struggle between opposing forces!" one student replied.

"Exactly," I responded, "and you are surrounded by conflict." After giving them a few minutes for observation, I asked the students for some

---

Figure 10.2. Journal Prompt

Outdoors today, find a spot of your own. Use your five senses to observe all that is happening around you. Write a list of what you see, hear, feel, and smell. Then use your notes to compose a poem, song, or paragraph that captures the moment.

Figure 10.3. Conflict

With your partner, observe elements of nature around you. Identify a conflict involving nature and complete the following activities. Write in complete sentences.

1. What are the two or more things that are in conflict?

2. Conflict is struggle. Briefly tell what the conflict you have observed is about.

3. Think about what will happen in this conflict. Write a paragraph to explain your prediction about how the struggle will develop and what outcome might end the conflict.

---

examples. They were at first confused and skeptical, because when children think of this term they tend to think of open physical conflict, like war. One student finally said, "Well, the flag wants to stay still, but the wind tries to move it."

"You're right," I said. "That is conflict, but the flag doesn't really want anything. The conflict is between the gravity pulling the flag and the wind blowing against it." After this exchange, the students started to look more closely at the world around them.

"What about gravity acting on a leaf?" someone asked. Now students felt more confident. Working in pairs, they were amazed at the number of conflicts going on all around them. At the end of the period one student said, "Okay, here's another conflict: you say we have to stop, but we really don't want to."

At other times the objective may be to observe some process in nature or to learn the names and ways of local wildlife. Although nature is magical, it is not like magic. Knowing how a trick is done diminishes it, but knowing how a cricket makes noise increases our appreciation. Writers use their knowledge of nature to make a pretend world believable.

For a lesson on integrating the naturalist's knowledge in writing I have used Diane Siebert's *Mojave,* a long poem illustrated by Wendell Minor.

First I read the poem aloud, and we list the many plants and animals mentioned. *Mojave* is perfect because it personifies the desert, a habitat that contrasts with our mid-Atlantic suburban setting. Siebert's work demonstrates the value of naming and clearly describing specific plants and animals. The following day's outdoor trek then gives us a chance to look for and identify Maryland wildlife. The planning and rules are the same as for our other outdoor excursions, but this time I bring along a canvas bag filled with field guides, including the wonderful Peterson First Guide series (published by Houghton Mifflin), as well as several Golden Guides (published by Golden Books). Students work in pairs, looking up various plants and trees in the guides. Usually we observe without collecting, because in the course of one day 140 students could defoliate a tree! For the teacher of writing, lessons like this offer many rewards. In stories and poems students will start to write *sparrow* or *robin* instead of simply *bird,* and even more important, they will start to care about the difference.

A Sense of Delight

Rachel Carson once wrote that a gift she would give to every child is a sense of wonder about the natural world. Emily Dickinson wrote, "If I read a book and it makes my whole body so cold no fire can ever warm me, I know that is poetry" (1991, p. 515). These ideas are closely akin, for they speak to the issue of emotion. Children feel first and ask questions after. The breathless "oooh" of a child seeing the ocean for the first time captures that sense of awe, the ability to be surprised by immensity. Children watching classmates perform the balcony scene in *Romeo and Juliet* often utter that same "oooh." It is the role of a teacher to treasure and nurture the ability of students to feel awe, to know delight, and to embrace experience. Teaching outside provides the perfect environment to link emotion to ideas.

That September morning as my students were outside, writing about the value of trees, is a case in point. The short story "Autumntime" by A. Lentini takes place in a world without trees. The narrator of the story, a child, has been taken on an excursion to see the last tree on the East Coast of the United States. He compares the real tree to the artificial ones he sees every day and decides that the real tree is much more intricate than the plastic ones. Before we read the story, we sit under our tree to write. We stay outside as we read the story and imagine a world without trees. The students talk in groups, and many share stories about trees they have known—a favorite tree to climb, a tree to read under, a tree that was a home to birds.

At one time, I might simply have used the story as an example of science fiction. Now it serves as a springboard for discussion about environmental issues. At the end of the story, the boy reveals that he has saved a single acorn from the last tree. He seems unaware that it is a seed. My students are usually intrigued by the possibilities suggested in the story. We try sprouting acorns and dissecting them. One student decided that since the boy didn't have access to real dirt, he might have tried to grow the acorn in water, so we filled a small cup with tap water, dropped in the acorn, and waited. It didn't work for us; but what was important was the process: we examined the science in the story and wondered how accurate the author was.

Students' written responses to the story revealed an emotional response to trees. Shannon, for example, composed a poem:

Reborn
An acorn falls upon the ground
The winds don't whisper; there is no sound.
The kids come running and jumping around
They stop to pick up what they've found.
They plant it in the soft moist soil.
Just sun, water, and love; no oil.
It will grow up brave and strong
As long as nothing goes wrong.
Through the years the kids will come
And play and swing and have fun.
Though the kids who planted it will still remember
Even when they bring their kids in September.
An acorn fell upon the ground
And a whole new life was then reborn.

Like all teachers, I reflect on my classroom practices. Does this type of teaching take too much time? Would it be better simply to analyze plot, setting, character, and theme? What are our objectives, and have they been met? There will never be enough time. Accepting that, I make every minute count. To teach language arts is to value words spoken, read, and written. When I take time to have my students look at a tree before we read, I provide them with a concrete experience that they can link to abstract ideas. Moreover, these activities can help students find the words to describe their experience. Standing beneath an oak tree on a fair autumn day is the perfect place to learn the word *translucent,* and light will never look more lovely than it does to me when we see it through the oak leaves. This is time well spent. And when I hear a student say, "I love this tree," I know that he or she will be able to write something that someone will read and love, too.

Forging the Link

By the end of the year, students no longer see activities as science or language arts; we read and write, question and test, and somehow it all works. Our class reflects life itself; there is not a separate compartment for activities.

This form of curricular integration offers authenticity and freedom. It encourages students to see literature on several levels, and it avoids limiting the class to rote repetition of literary terms. Furthermore, integrating science and writing affords students opportunities to practice science writing techniques in writing workshop.

The best reason to integrate science and language arts is the model provided by practicing scientists. Our classroom saying is "It doesn't matter what you find out if you don't write it down." This motto would apply just as well to a science class—or to a nuclear physics lab. Students who learn to write for real purposes value writing. Because they use writing to communicate their own ideas, they want to be clear, and because they want others to accept their ideas, they want to be correct. Since I have been providing students with authentic reasons for writing I have found that they write longer pieces, not because they have to, but because they have much to say.

Why is my class outside? Maybe a student's words give the best answer: "By experiencing so many things outdoors, I felt different than I would in school. With so many things to observe outside I felt alert. Everywhere I looked there was something new. I felt like I could stay outside all day and not see everything." No filmstrip, no video, no picture can ever capture the real experience of being outdoors—where the individual student decides where to look and for how long to watch, where sounds are layered one upon the other, where even the air on one's skin feels somehow different from the air indoors. We go outside because there the sun beckons and the wind sings. We go outside to learn, and to write about the world.

Annotated Bibliography

Bradbury, Ray. "December 2001: The Green Morning." I found this story in a Ginn anthology entitled *The Study of Literature*. The story is dated, but is still interesting and raises some great questions because it occurs on Mars. If you planted trees on Mars, would you get oxygen?

Crane, Stephen. "War." This story can be found in several anthologies, including Harcourt, Brace, and Jovanovich's *Adventures in Reading* (1980 ed.). I use it to focus on sensory imagery. Caution: within the text there are brief descriptions of bloodstains and other results of armed conflict. Although in our society such descriptions are part of everyday life, the teacher should be sensitive about use of this material. "War" is best suited for students who are in middle school or beyond.

Dowden, Anne Ophelia. *The Clover and the Bee: A Book of Pollination.* New York: HarperCollins, 1990.
Students need models of clear explanatory writing; this is one. Dowden links beautiful pictures to well-written text in a description of a process that students can readily observe.

Johnson, Cathy. *The Sierra Club Guide to Sketching in Nature.* San Francisco: Sierra Club Books, 1990.
I have students sketch in my class several times during the year. This book is way beyond my artistic ability, but it contains some helpful ideas for any teacher who wants to sharpen students' observation skills.

Van Matre, Steve, and Bill Weiler, eds. *The Earth Speaks: Acclimatization Journal.* Cedar Grove, WV: The Institute for Earth Education, 1983.
Much of the best writing of the twentieth century has centered on the environment for the same reason that children's writing about nature is often so compelling: the pen writes best what the heart feels. This collection is food for the soul. I use quotes from the text in my classroom to spark persuasive writing, and I read it at home, often, because I never tire of it.

Resources

The Elementary Science Integration Project

The following are books and videos by and about the Elementary Science Integration Project (ESIP) and its participants and staff. Consult the ESIP web site at <http://www.umbc.edu/esip> for further information.

Bourne, Barbara, and Wendy Saul. 1994. *Exploring Space: Using Seymour Simon's Astronomy Books in the Classroom*. New York: Morrow Junior Books.

Elementary Science Integration Project. 1995. *Thinking Science*. Video. Directed by Joyce Green. Portsmouth, NH: Heinemann.

———. 1996. *How to Write an Ecological Mystery with Jean Craighead George*. Video. Directed by Twig George. Annapolis, MD: Walkabout Productions.

Pearce, Charles. 1999. *Nurturing Inquiry: Real Science for the Elementary Classroom*. Portsmouth, NH: Heinemann.

Saul, Wendy, et al. 1993. *Science Workshop: A Whole Language Approach*. Portsmouth, NH: Heinemann.

Saul, Wendy, and Jeanne Reardon, eds. 1996. *Beyond the Science Kit: Inquiry in Action*. Portsmouth, NH: Heinemann.

Resources for Teachers

Atwell, Nancie. 1987. *In the Middle: Writing, Reading, and Learning with Adolescents*. Portsmouth, NH: Heinemann.

Carson, Rachel. 1956. *The Sense of Wonder*. New York: Harper & Row.

Cerullo, Mary M. 1997. *Reading the Environment: Children's Literature in the Science Classroom*. Portsmouth, NH: Heinemann.

Firehock, Karen. 1994. *Hands on Save Our Streams*. Gaithersburg, MD: Izaak Walton League of America.

Hogan, Kathleen. 1994. *Eco-Inquiry*. Dubuque, IA: Kendall Hunt Publishing.

Lieberman, Gerald, and Linda Hoody. 1998. *Closing the Achievement Gap: Using the Environment as an Integrated Context for Learning*. Poway, CA: Science Wizards.

National Aquarium in Baltimore. 1987. *Living in Water: An Aquatic Science Curriculum for Grades 4–6.* Baltimore, MD: The National Aquarium.

National Science Education Standards. 1996. Washington, DC: National Academy Press.

National Science Resources Center. 1996. *Ecosytems Teacher's Guide.* Burlington, NC: Carolina Biological Supply.

Project WILD Aquatic Education Activity Guide. 1992. Bethesda, MD: Project WILD.

Project WILD K–12 Activity Guide. 1992. Bethesda, MD: Project WILD.

Resources for Teaching Elementary School Science. 1996. Washington, DC: National Academy Press.

Rivkin, Mary S. 1995. *The Great Outdoors: Restoring Children's Right to Play Outside.* Washington, DC: NAEYC.

Slattery, Britt. 1995. *WOW! The Wonders of Wetlands: An Educator's Guide.* Baltimore, MD: De Vilbiss Printing.

Williams, Paul H. 1993. *Bottle Biology.* Dubuque, IA: Kendall Hunt Publishing.

Field Guide Series for Children

Golden Guides. Golden Books.

National Audubon Society First Field Guides. New York: Scholastic.

Peterson Field Guides for Young Naturalists. Boston: Houghton Mifflin.

Web Sites

Audubon Society:
    <http://www.audubon.org/educate>

Burtonsville Elementary School:
    <http://www3.mcps.k12.md.us/schools/burtonsivllees/>

Chesapeake Bay Trust:
    <http://www2.ari.net/cbt/wwwhome.html>

Council for Environmental Education (CEE) (includes Project WILD, Project WET, Project Learning Tree, and Project Learning Tree in the City):
    <http://www.projectwild.org> or contact National Program Manager, Project Learning Tree, 1111 19th St. NW, Suite 780, Washington, DC 20036. (202-463-2462).

Environmental Protection Agency resources for teachers:
    <http://www.epa.gov/teachers/>

Montgomery County DEP:
    <http://www.co.mo.md.us/dep/>

North American Association for Environmental Education:
    <http://www.naaee.org>

Roger Tory Peterson Institute programs for teachers:
   <http://www.rtpi.org>
Save Our Streams (Izaak Walton League of America):
   <http://www.people.Virginia.EDU/~sos-iwla/Stream-
   Study/StreamStudyHomePage/StreamStudy.HTML>
State Education and Environment Roundtable:
   <http://www.seer.org>
USGS Learning Web:
   <http:/www.usgs.gov/education/learnweb>
Westbrook Elementary School:
   <http://www.mcps.k12.md.us/schools/westbrookes/>

Works Cited

Arnosky, James. 1983. *Secrets of a Wildlife Watcher*. New York: Lothrop, Lee and Shepard.

Atwell, Nancie. 1987. *In the Middle: Writing, Reading, and Learning with Adolescents*. Portsmouth, NH: Heinemann.

Carson, Rachel. 1956. *The Sense of Wonder*. New York: Harper & Row.

Dewey, Jennifer Owings. 1987. *At the Edge of the Pond*. Boston: Little, Brown.

———. 1991. *Animal Architecture*. New York: Orchard Books.

Dickinson, Emily. 1991. In *Literature Gold*. Englewood Cliffs, NJ: Prentice Hall.

George, Jean Craighead. 1983. *The Talking Earth*. New York: Harper & Row.

———. 1995. *Everglades*. New York: HarperCollins.

Hughes, Langston. 1988. "April Rain Song." In Beatrice Schenk de Regniers, ed., *Sing a Song of Popcorn: Every Child's Book of Poems*. New York: Scholastic.

Johnson, Mary Beth. 1996. "Looking for Hope in All the Wrong Places." In Wendy Saul and Jeanne Reardon, eds., *Beyond the Science Kit: Inquiry in Action*. Portsmouth, NH: Heinemann.

Lentini, A. 1989. "Autumntime." In Gail Dristle, *Literature*. New York: McDougal Littell.

Macaulay, David. 1976. *Underground*. Boston: Houghton Mifflin.

Moore, Lillian. 1992. "In the Fog." In X. J. Kennedy and Dorothy M. Kennedy, eds., *Talking Like the Rain: A Read-to-Me Book of Poems*. Boston: Little, Brown.

National Science Education Standards. 1996. Washington, DC: National Academy Press.

Pearce, Charles. 1993. "What If . . . ?" In Wendy Saul et al., *Science Workshop: A Whole Language Approach*. Portsmouth, NH: Heinemann.

Saul, Wendy, et al. 1993. *Science Workshop: A Whole Language Approach*. Portsmouth, NH: New Hampshire.

Saul, Wendy, and Jeanne Reardon, eds. 1996. *Beyond the Science Kit: Inquiry in Action*. Portsmouth, NH: Heinemann.

Siebert, Diane. 1992. *Mojave*. New York: HarperCollins.

Thoreau, Henry David. 1997. *Walden*. Boston: Beacon Press. (Orig. pub. Boston: Ticknor and Fields, 1854.)

Wilson, Edward O. 1994. *Naturalist*. Washington, DC: Warner Books.

Yeats, William Butler. 1928. "Among School Children." In *The Tower*. New York: Macmillan.